The Prestonpans Tapestry 1745

Created by Andrew Crummy, Dorie Wilkie, Gillian Hart,
Gordon Prestoungrange and 'The Stitchers'

Burke's Peerage & Gentry

ISBN 978-0-85011-121-7 (hardback)
ISBN 978-0-85011-122-4 (paperback)

Prestoungrange University Press with Burke's Peerage & Gentry for
The Battle of Prestonpans 1745 Heritage Trust
227/229 High Street, Prestonpans
East Lothian, Scotland EH32 9BE

Design & Typesetting by Chat Noir Design, France
Printed & bound in Great Britain

Contents

iv

Foreword

It's an incredible story. If an author submitted it as fiction, a publisher would reject it as too improbable to be believable.

A prince descends upon a remote Scottish island with just seven followers – well, slightly more than that, but not enough to matter – with the dream of reclaiming his exiled father's crown. He raises his banner, and within weeks an army springs up, threatens a throne, and would probably have toppled it too, had the dream not been squelched at Derby by the cramped vision of his principal lieutenants. But before that dream turns sour, he mounts a masterful military campaign, destroys an opposing army, conquers one of his father's three former kingdoms (Scotland) and penetrates to the very heart of another, the most powerful of the three (England), to the point where he has its capital within his grasp. The prince's confidence, driving ambition, and certainty of his own rectitude and the rectitude of his cause had proved contagious. And self fulfilling.

A fairy tale, yes? But it isn't. This tale is real. Who, with soul alive to romance, could resist its allure?

I was drawn to the tale in a round-about way. Tales of this sort typically include a villain, or, if not a villain, a "fall guy," or foil, whose iniquities or follies make the hero's exploits shine more brilliantly in contrast. The villain/fall guy/foil of this story was General Sir John Cope, British Commander-in-Chief in Scotland. Cope had the misfortune to command the inexperienced army that the Prince – I refer, of course, to Charles Edward Stuart – routed in less than fifteen minutes on the morning of 21 September, 1745, at what came to be known as the Battle of Prestonpans, named for a nearby East Lothian village. (Was it at 5 a.m.? at 6 a.m.? Accounts differ, as they differ about so much else concerning the battle, including what to name it.) For two-and-a-half centuries thereafter, history and folklore alike had, with only rare dissenting voices, cast the luckless general as a buffoon. But then I acquired, for more money than I ever let

on to my wife, the transcript of an official Inquiry into Cope's conduct. And, lo, the Inquiry concluded that Cope was blameless – rightly so in my judgement, which I base largely on the voluminous evidence that the Inquiry Board uncovered.

What standing had I to make such a judgement, when I had never served in any army, let alone an eighteenth-century British one? Ah, but I have been a lawyer, a human rights lawyer, most of my life, and it seems to me that courtroom combat can resemble real combat (except that the former is perhaps fractionally more civilized). In particular, one can plan meticulously, and make all the right decisions, only to have one's plans collapse because of some unforeseeable occurrence, as when a key witness unexpectedly changes his story. So too with Cope: he had anticipated every contingency except for one that he could neither have foreseen nor prevented – that his army, in high spirits only moments earlier, would panic, collapse and run in the face of the dreaded highland charge.

The human rights lawyer in me was hooked – Cope had been unjustly vilified over the centuries, and I would strive henceforward to rehabilitate him. So I immersed myself in the tale and wrote, first a magazine article, then a book, in which I defended the general's behavior.

By coincidence, at the same time that I was researching and writing the book, Gordon Wills – who was then unknown to me – had purchased land, adjacent to the Prestonpans battlefield, which belonged to the old Prestoungrange feudal barony. In short order he assumed the title and became Gordon Prestoungrange, established the Battle of Prestonpans Heritage Trust, and launched an ambitious campaign to conserve, interpret and present the battlefield – both as a worthy undertaking for its own sake and as a means of bringing tourism and income to one of Scotland's most depressed communities. The Trust's many projects have included creating a press to publish non-fiction and fiction about the '45;

establishing the Alan Breck "regiment" to participate in battle re-enactments (Breck, immortalized in Robert Louis Stevenson's "Kidnapped," was a real figure who had fought in the British army before deserting to the Jacobites; appropriately the regiment, of which I was gazetted as honorary "colonel," provides re-enactors to both sides); and encouraging noted battlefield archaeologist Tony Pollard to do field research on, and under, the battle site. Already Tony's conclusions have unseated long-held notions about the battle, including some of mine – though they have not shaken my belief in Cope's innocence. And, enlisting the services of renowned artist Andrew Crummy and of a veritable army of volunteers, the Trust has commissioned a tapestry – emulator and rival of its famous prototype from Bayeux – that traces every step of the Prestonpans campaign from the Prince's departure from Rome and France to the battle's immediate aftermath.

Some tales drag on for too long. Charlie's own legend would have been better served if he had perished at Culloden or in the heather; what followed was sad, even sordid, and truly does not bear re-telling. So it is as well that the tapestry ends with the Jacobite army victorious at Prestonpans and poised to conquer England – before the dream turned sour. The world has seen enough of sad endings.

There will be no sad ending to the Battle Heritage Trust's many projects. For today's feudal Baron, if his modesty will permit me to say so, has much in common with Charles Edward. He raises his banner (in the figurative sense; literally, he parks his now-famous Battle Bus), and an army of volunteers springs up, just as it did for Charlie. This army is equipped, not with Lochaber axes and pitchforks, as many of Charlie's soldiers were, but with assorted talents and above all with unquenchable enthusiasm – for the Baron Gordon's confidence, ambition, and belief in his cause are contagious and self fulfilling: the same as Charlie's. And while these volunteers have neither toppled nor even threatened a throne (although some might like to), they have, *inter alia* as lawyers say, written books, staged re-enactments, and constructed a tapestry that emulates and rivals its famous prototype from Bayeux — all in pursuance of their dream of perpetuating the memory of that earlier dream. But this dream will not turn sour.

Martin Margulies
July 2010

The Tapestry Background

The saga of Prince Charles Edward's campaign in 1745 is as enduring as that of William the Bastard, Duke of Normandy and King of England from 1066. Both sought to recover a nation's crown that had been snatched away from them by 'usurpers'.

William had been usurped by Harold despite his knowing full well that King Edward the Confessor had originally bequeathed the throne to William. The Stuart's direct line of male descent suffered serial usurpation. They were first displaced by the Act of Settlement in the English Parliament because the Prince's grandfather King James II and VII was a Catholic, his second wife was a Catholic and their male heir had just been born in 1688. There was no appetite in England for Catholicism at that time and thenceforth Catholics were barred from all right to sit upon the throne. The male Catholic Stuart line was displaced in favour first of the female children of James II and VII's first marriage to Protestant Anne Hyde. The eldest daughter became Queen Mary II [1689-1694] and her husband, a Dutch Prince, joint sovereign as William III and II [1689-1702]; and they were succeeded by Queen Mary's younger sister who became Queen Anne [1702-1714]. Thereafter, since Queen Anne had no children, the Electors of Hanover, distant Protestant cousins, took the crown as direct descendants of Elizabeth, sister of the Stuart King Charles I whom Parliament had executed in 1649.

There were several bold attempts most particularly in 1689 and 1715 to restore the male Stuart line in the person of James II and VII himself and his son James III and VIII – the Old Pretender. But none came so near to success as the campaign James III and VIII's son Prince Charles Edward, *aka* Bonnie Prince Charlie or the Young Pretender, waged in 1745.

La Tapisserie de la Reine Mathilde

The success of King William I of England at Hastings in 1066 was at great cost in battle, and the Pope required of William that as penance he build an Abbey part of which survived Henry VIII's Dissolution and stands to this day on the field where King Harold was slain – at Battle in Sussex. William's wife, Queen Mathilde went further however to oversee the creation of one of the world's most famous works of art – the Bayeux Tapestry also known as *La Tapisserie de la Reine Mathilde*. Under the supervision of William's half-brother, Earl of Kent and Bishop Odo of Bayeux [some say it was the inspiration of the late King Harold's ambitious sister Edith], 230 feet by twenty inches of the finest embroidery was stitched. It tells the saga of usurpation and William's 'just' invasion to secure his inheritance. It was created [probably at Canterbury] to decorate the walls of Bishop Odo's newly consecrated Cathedral of Bayeux in 1077 – just 11 years after William's Victory. The tapestry has never left France and it has only left Bayeux twice. On both occasions it was to be exhibited in Paris – firstly to celebrate the proclamation of Napoleon I as Emperor in 1804, and secondly to celebrate France's Liberation in 1944 – which had appropriately arrived through Normandy.

Much more has certainly been written about the '45 and the role Prince Charles Edward and the Highland Clan Chiefs played in it than of William at Hastings, but until 2008 embroidery on the scale of Bayeux had not been envisaged to tell of his saga. The belief that it could and should be accomplished followed a chance visit to Bayeux by members of the Battle of Prestonpans 1745 Heritage Trust allied to Prestonpans growing reputation as an emerging centre for community arts. The arts in myriad forms whether painting, poetry, writing, music, singing, sculpture, story telling or theatre had for a decade been a deliberate vehicle for post-industrial socioeconomic regeneration of Prestonpans under the umbrella of the Prestoungrange Arts Festival Trust. Furthermore, their focus had been the millennium history of the town – since William the Conqueror in fact. In turn the Viking and monastic origins of the town, its early coal mining and salt making, its oyster farming, its glassworks and chemical industries, its potteries, its soap making and brewing, its market gardening and brick making were all honoured in mural art. The town's sad record of witch persecution in the reigns of Queen Mary and James VI was commemorated in theatre and literature. And from 2006

Prince Charles Edward's astonishing Victory in the town has been honoured too.

Researching the Prince's Campaign

It was apparent from the outset to members of the Prestoungrange Arts Festival that appropriate conservation, interpretation and presentation of the Battle of Prestonpans on September 21st 1745 was a matter for the Scottish nation at large. Panners, indwellers of Prestonpans, are but stewards of the legacy. Accordingly a discrete Battle of Prestonpans 1745 Heritage Trust was founded which has always seen its responsibility was to involve the whole nation, building nevertheless on the abundant strengths of the town's arts community. The occasional remembrance of the battle, at 100th, 200th and 250th anniversaries had been successful but the Trust believed a permanent, living history approach was proper for the 21st century. Accordingly to address that *Dream*, for that was what we chose to call it, we began with an audit of all that had been essayed across the previous 265 years. This included the works of artists, the novels of Scott and Stephenson and hundreds more, the poetry and the songs and anthems sung, the films and videos, the local memorials to Colonel Gardiner and the thorn tree beneath which he was mortally wounded, the cairn where many of those who died were finally laid to rest, the BattleBing that stands at Meadow Mill just north of the A1 Great North Road close by the battle site with panoramic views of the entire sequence of manoeuvres by both armies, the contemporary diaries and memoirs, the Proceedings of the Court of Enquiry Field Marshal Wade convened that exonerated Sir John Cope for his crushing defeat, the Trial of Lord Provost Stuart of Edinburgh, and finally the researches and opinions of hundreds of historians across the intervening years. In this latter respect the Trust was especially fortunate that a US human rights lawyer, Martin Margulies, with a holiday home on South Uist close by Eriskay where the Prince first landed on 23rd July 1745, had brought his analytical skills to the same task as the Trustees. In the very same year that the Battle Trust was launched Martin Margulies published the first and only scholarly work exclusively devoted to, and entitled, *The Battle of Prestonpans 1745*.

Martin Margulies's study, and Stephen Lord's work In *Walking With Charlie*, which reported how Lord had walked the very route the Prince had taken through the Highlands in 1745, became the prime sources for the events depicted in the The Prestonpans Tapestry as pictured on the pages of this book. But the tapestry also tells of Sir John Cope's unsuccessful attempt to head off the Prince in the Highlands in July and August and of the barges he took from Aberdeen to Dunbar – too late to save Edinburgh but

sufficient to place his army between the Prince and England in mid September and ready for battle at Prestonpans.

Another distinguished scholar has also supported the Trust's work. With a grant from the Heritage Lottery Dr Tony Pollard and colleagues from Glasgow University's Battlefield Archaeology Centre have conducted a careful examination of the battle site and been able to suggest that, from artefacts found, the precise location of the initial clash was close by Seton Farm East. They have also been able to evaluate the gravity Waggonway that ran across the subsequent field of battle, carrying coal downhill from Tranent to Cockenzie Harbour – which was indeed Scotland's first railway.

Living History in Action

A significant programme of annual September re-enactments of known cameos of the battle was instituted in 2007 with the support of appropriately uniformed volunteers from the Czech Republic, Holland, Ireland, Wales, England and of course Scotland itself. The re-enactors dined at Holyroodhouse Palace. In Prestonpans an extensive mural was painted at the town's primary school. Under the leadership of 'Colonel' Adam Watters with the support of the Pipes and Drums of the Royal British Legion, the Alan Breck Regiment of Prestonpans Volunteers has been raised. Martin Margulies became its first 'Colonel-in-Chief'. A young man precisely the same age as the Prince in 1745, Arran Johnston, has role-played the Prince himself since the outset. All the local battle scenes depicted on the tapestry panels have been re-enacted to the ever growing enjoyment of the community of Prestonpans and visitors from afar. On the occasion of The Gathering and Scotland's Homecoming in 2009 the Trust's Exhibition of The Princes' Clans who came out at Prestonpans attracted descendants from as far away as New Zealand.

Theatre has made a major contribution with two plays from Aberlady born BAFTA Winner Andrew Dallmeyer – *The Battle of Pots 'n Pans* which toured and went on to the Edinburgh Fringe, and *Colonel Gardiner – Vice and Virtue*. So too has the encouragement of novelists under the local Cuthill Press imprint to create new novels, with Sharon Dabell's *A Backward Glance* and Roy Pugh's *The White Rose and the Thorn Tree*. Gordon Prestoungrange has also contributed his own novel, *A Baron's Tale*, telling of William Grant's involvement at the time and later as Lord Advocate.

In 2009 the Trust received a grant from the Scottish Arts Council and Awards for All that enabled Greg Dawson-Allen to become Story Teller of the Battle taking the tale to schools across the county and beyond. In the programme of School Visits he was joined by Adam Watters and by local resident Gordon Veitch, twice European BattleGaming Champion. On behalf of the Trust Gordon Veitch has constructed a 10ft x 8 ft topographical representation of Prestonpans and the battlefield in 1745. On the boards by the throw of the dice Cope and the Prince do battle once again and annual championship competitions are arranged.

Designing and Stitching The Prestonpans Tapestry

Andrew Crummy, Convenor of the Prestoungrange Arts Festival for most of the decade, was the principal artist and illustrator of the tapestry. The stitching of the embroidery was led by Dorie Wilkie. The whole was co-ordinated administratively by Gillian Hart who was also the principal photographer. The stitching was shared across Scotland and around the world by more than 200 volunteers each of whom has their tag in the bottom right hand corner of their panel. Recruiting the stitchers was undertaken in the initial stages by Sylvia Burgess. Webmaster was Gordon Prestoungrange.

Andrew Crummy is an accomplished artist in many media and at an early stage in his life worked as an illustrator. As such he was not daunted by the challenge to create all the artwork for the many panels to a consistent style. But what style to choose? He began with the famous 18th century cartoon of Cope confirming his own defeat to Lord Kerr at Berwick on Tweed and developed that. He created black pencil sketches which were then subject to 'sign off' wherever possible in the communities across Scotland where the Prince and Cope travelled. He was determined that each locality should make its own contribution, and tell its own version of the events depicted. This was never more important than when several versions were abroad, such as where precisely at Glenfinnan was the Prince's standard raised and by whom? Or which rose bush at Fassfern was the origin of the white cockade? Equally it was important to seek to find the 18th century exteriors of buildings many since demolished such as the Netherbow Port and Preston House; derelict as at High Bridge and Ruthven Barracks; or extensively altered such as Blair Castle, Balhaldie House, Kinlochmoidart House, the Salutation Inn in Perth, the Cottage at Duddingston and Tranent Church. To assist all this, focussed book and internet research and seemingly endless cross-examination of Martin Margulies lasted for fully nine months. Architect Gareth Bryn-Jones was deeply involved, on occasions 'estimating' how a building might have appeared mid-18th century. Field visits around the Highlands were arranged in village halls and centres, most particularly at

Eriskay, Arisaig, Borrodale, Glenfinnan, High Bridge, Ruthven, Blair Castle and Dunblane.

Next there was the question of which wools to use to create a tapestry that could last a thousand years and on which linen to embroider it. Andrew Crummy knew he wanted subdued Scottish hues, but the red coats of the Hanoverian government's troops were often in danger of dominating the panels. Panel stitchers were also invited to networking workshops and 'problem clinics', with senior stitchers across the country assisting closer to the work in hand. A core team led by Dorie Wilkie also addressed the challenge of sewing the panels together since each is embroidered separately; and the most appropriate backing for the linen and how best to hang it in exhibition – for which Velcro was adopted.

The question was sometimes raised as to whether such a project could be accomplished in just 24 months from start to exhibition. The Trust took the view of Adam Smith that, so long as there was a division of labour, it could. But with post-Smithsonian managerial insight, the questions raised by the logistics of supporting such widely dispersed stitchers and the eventual challenge of a touring exhibition were addressed by a special task group. Nodes on the critical path were identified and resourced as appropriate to avoid bottlenecks.

Why stop at the Prince's Victory in Prestonpans?

Unlike William I of England, the Prince's campaign was not ultimately crowned with success. At Culloden the Prince and the Highland Clans were defeated. The Hanoverian government went on the ensure that the loyalty and support on which the Prince had been able to draw for his success were destroyed for ever. At Westminster they even banned the wearing of the tartan and playing of the pipes. Yet paradoxically in so doing they created the abiding and romanticised myth of the Prince, and provided a touchstone for much that is universally recognised as distinctive about Scotland today – not least those 'illegal' tartans and the pipes.

The National Trust for Scotland has most recently created a major new visitor centre at Culloden that tells the comprehensive and turbulent Jacobite story. It began when Henry VIII's sister married the Scottish King and shows how this eventually led by male descent after the death of Queen Elizabeth I to the ascension to the throne of England of Scotland's then ruling King James VI, the son of Mary Queen of Scots. His son, Charles I, lost his head to Parliament, and following the interregnum with the two Cromwells as Lord Protector, King Charles II and then his brother James II and VII ruled before the 'Glorious Revolution' saw James abdicate and flee into exile. It continues with the tales of the Uprisings from 1689 till 1746 and then to the end of the lives of Prince Charles Edward and his younger brother Cardinal Prince Henry in Rome. In so doing, in telling the whole story, the significance of the Prince's campaign to Victory at Prestonpans all too frequently gets lost amidst myriad other details. In Prestonpans it is our particular ambition to ensure that does not happen.

It is our conviction and belief in Prestonpans that the Prince's quite extraordinary campaign leading to his Victory on September 21st 1745 can be and should be exemplified in its own right.

A young man of 24 turning 25 arrived with 7 supporters in the Outer Hebrides full of Hope and Ambition. From that seemingly improbable start, advised to "Go Home" immediately on arrival, he wrote letters to Clan Chiefs from Borrodale House, raised his Standard at Glenfinnan after less than a month to be joined there first by Cameron of Lochiel and then a further 2000 Clansmen. He took Edinburgh some eight weeks after landing. He had Scotland at his feet and defeated Cope at Prestonpans in an astonishing encounter that lasted no more than fifteen minutes.

It is our assertion in Prestonpans today that Prince Charles Edward set an example every young person can seek to follow in their lives. He identified what he believed to be right, he committed himself to it completely, he motivated older and wiser men than he to join him, and he achieved Victory. The fact that the later stages of his campaign failed was no justification for not striving for what he believed to be right. True there is a moral to the story in that his timing was right to begin, and would have been right to have pressed ahead from Derby even though the promised support from France was delayed. But once he had turned back from Derby there was never any hope he might have succeeded. So timing and retaining the initiative are perhaps the abiding lessons to be internalised.

Hope, Ambition & Victory are synonymous with Prestonpans – then and now

So to the final question asked. It is one which, if The Trust had worried unduly about its answer would have ensured embroidering the tapestry never began.

Where is our soon to be consecrated cathedral of Bayeux provided by the Earl of Kent Bishop Odo, half-brother to the Bastard Duke, the conquering King William I? Where will *we* display The Prestonpans Tapestry when completed? Will the Lord provide?

The Trust's answer is both straightforward and ambitious. We expect it to hang in the future Prestonpans Living History Centre which is not yet constructed nor even funded. But when it is, as it surely will be, The Prestonpans Tapestry will be one of its key exhibits that will bring thousands of visitors, young children in particular, to Prestonpans to hear and learn exactly what the 24 turning 25 year old Prince achieved in just eight weeks.

Battle Trustee, architect and artist Gareth Bryn-Jones has worked with structural engineers and internationally acclaimed interior designers *haleysharpe* to explore and present how the Living History Centre can ideally be created as an extension of the BattleBing already in place. There are several alternative locations such as the town's extensive Heritage Museum which the Trust is also considering. In the meantime however, it is the Trust's intention to 'parade' The Prestonpans Tapestry far and wide, anywhere and everywhere audiences are interested to hear its message of Youthful Hope and Ambition and just precisely what Victory can be achieved.

Our message has been derided by a few thoughtful critics as delusional, as denying the ultimate reality of the Prince's campaign i.e. that it failed. We absolutely beg to differ in post-industrial Prestonpans. The fact that *'the best laid schemes o' mice an' men gang aft agley"* never was or ever shall be an alibi for not striving in a positive frame of mind to achieve what is important to one's life. Hundreds of hands moving to a shared goal across the Scottish nation have made the point. They have stitched for more than 15,000 hours to create the world's longest embroidered artwork at 104 metres – The Prestonpans Tapestry. Their stunning creation shall surely be our beacon for generations to come.

Dr Gordon Prestoungrange
Baron of Prestoungrange
Chairman: Battle of Prestonpans 1745 Heritage Trust

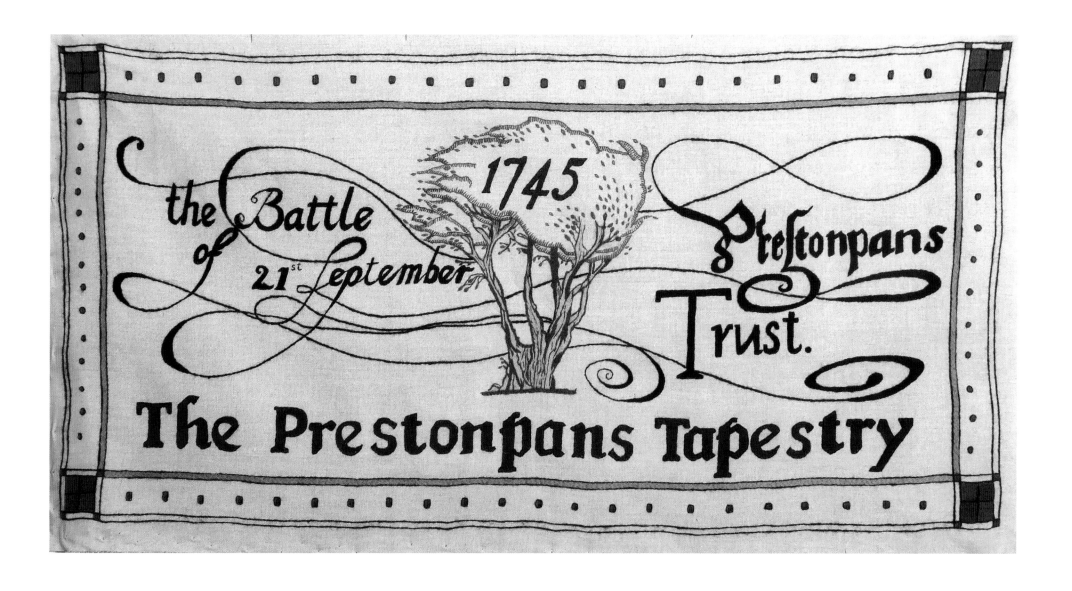

The Battle
of
21st September
1745

Prestonpans
Trust.

The Prestonpans Tapestry

Embroidered by Elma Colvin for the Prestonpans 1745 Heritage Trust

1 Charles bids farewell in Rome to his father, King James VIII & III

By 1744 the French had decided to invade the United Kingdom. Learning of this Charles resolved to take the opportunity to restore his father King James VIII and III to his throne. He took leave of his father in Rome as follows:

"I go, Sire, in search of three crowns, which I doubt not but to have the honour and happiness of laying at Your Majesty's feet. If I fail in the attempt, your next sight of me shall be in a coffin." To which the King replied:

"Heaven forbid that all the crowns in the world should rob me of my son. Be careful of yourself, my dear Prince, for my sake and, I hope, for the sake of millions."

Officially he went hunting with his younger brother Henry. But in practice, defying the British spies, he slipped past the Royal Navy to reach Antibes then crossed France in just five days. He arrived in Paris to the consternation of King Louis XV who had not thus far seen his invasion as the occasion for the restoration of the Stuarts. So the Prince went incognito and soon joined the invasion force as 'Baron Douglas'.

This panel was created by Gillian Curtis-Hart from Leeds who has stayed in Port Seton since 2003. She has been deeply involved since then with the Prestonpans & Three Harbours Arts Festivals and soon became involved with the tapestry as its co-ordinator. But once she saw the astounding artworks and embroidery passing before her eyes she could not resist volunteering for herself. "Some weeks I couldn't put it down, others I couldn't pick it up. But with much help from fellow stitchers and despite sore fingers, eyes, and back I am deeply proud to have played a part in this amazing project".

Charles bids farewell in Rome to his father, King James VIII & III

2 Storms destroy the French invasion fleet in 1744 so Charles makes his own plans in secret

King Louis XV's invasion fleet was unfortunately scattered in two storms in February 1744 and that, coupled with the clear lack of enthusiasm at the French Court for a Stuart Restoration, led Prince Charles to conclude he must make his own plans. He fervently believed Scotland would rise so O'Sullivan was recruited to provide military expertise, and a loan of 180,000 livres was raised to purchase weapons and arrange ships. As Charles' confidence grew he flouted his incognito in Paris sitting close at a royal ball to the Queen, and deliberately attracting her attention. He struck up a warm relationship with some of his relatives, the du Bouillons. By early summer 1745 he and his closest associates were ready to rendez-vous secretly in Nantes. Their plans to raise the Highlands and reclaim the three crowns of Scotland, England and Ireland were now in place.

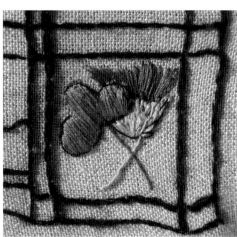

This panel was created by Linda Reid originally born in Carrickfergus, Northern Ireland of Scottish and Irish parents. "I have worked as a maternity nurse – dealing with new Mums and new babies never seems to lose its wonder for me. I felt sharing in the tapestry would be a 'once in a life time' opportunity to leave something to posterity and I've enjoyed the camaraderie of the group. Half way through my panel I went down with a very heavy cold so I placed the tapestry on the floor (for safety) whilst I made a *lemsip*. As I carried it back I promptly spilled the contents over the work ..... couldn't be saved, had to start again. Henceforth I've been known as '*lemsip* linda'. I have had much help from another Lynn so it's a tapestry of two Lynns, one Scots one Irish – hence the Thistle and Shamrock in my tag."

Storms destroy the French invasion fleet in 1744 so Charles makes his own plans in secret

3 The Prince Embarks from St Nazaire in France for Scotland aboard du Teillay – June 22nd

On June 21st 1745 Prince Charles personally made his way from Nantes to the quiet trading port at St Nazaire disguised as a student of the Scottish College in Paris. Here he was joined by seven immediate supporters who had travelled independently to avoid arousing attention. They were the Jacobite Duke of Atholl, Aeneas MacDonald, Francis Strickland, Sir Thomas Sheridan, George Kelly, Sir John MacDonald and John O'Sullivan. Also in the party were Abbe Butler and Duncan Cameron of Barra who knew the Hebridean seaways perfectly. The following day they boarded the 44 gun ship *du Teillay* and sailed to La Belle Isle to await their second vessel, *L'Elisabeth*, which was to carry soldiers, gold and munitions.

This panel was embroidered at Feuillade in France by Jenny Unwin. Her husband John is graphic designer of the tapestry guide book for Chat Noir Design. They are recent migrants to France and are converting their barn to start an art-based enterprise. She loves any type of stitching, particularly knitting, having run a successful small business designing and creating machine-knitted garments in England. Contributing to the tapestry as part of a much larger project has been a great pleasure.

22ND JUNE

NANTES

ST NAZAIRE

THE PRINCE EMBARKS FROM FRANCE FOR SCOTLAND ABOARD DU TEILLAY ST NAZAIRE

The Prince Embarks from St Nazaire in France for Scotland aboard du Teillay – June 22nd

4 700 French soldiers aboard L'Elisabeth join the Prince at La Belle Isle and they sail for Scotland – July 5th

On July 4th *L'Elisabeth*, a 64 gunner, arrived at La Belle Isle with more than 700 French soldiers, gold and munitions on board and the Prince was at last ready to make sail. On July 5th *du Teillay*, which now also had gold and munitions on board, and *L'Elisabeth*, sailed for Scotland under the command of Anthony Walsh [later Jacobite Earl Walsh] who had procured both ships for the Prince's journey on the instructions of Lord Clare. Almost 18 months after leaving Rome the Prince's hopes and ambition were to be put to the test. His campaign to regain his father's birthright had begun.

This panel was embroidered by Susan Meadows at Bayford in Hertfordshire. She is married with three children and has two granddaughters and has always enjoyed all kinds of handicrafts particularly knitting, sewing and dressmaking. Wedding and bridesmaids dresses have been a speciality. However this panel is her first embroidery work which she has greatly enjoyed. Like all the others she is very much looking forward to seeing the completed tapestry.

5th JULY
700 MEN
1500 MUSKETS
1800 BROADSWORD
CAPTAIN D'O
ANTOINE WALSH
DU TEILLAY
700 FRENCH SOLDIERS GO ABOARD L'ELISABETH AT LA BELLE ISLE WHICH SETS SAIL WITH DU TEILLAY
SM

panel 4

700 French soldiers aboard L'Elisabeth join the Prince at La Belle Isle and they sail for Scotland – July 5th

5 L'Elisabeth engages in sea battle with HMS Lion – July 9th

panel
5

On July 9th the 64 gun English man-of-war *HMS* Lion, commanded by Captain Percy Brett, intercepted *du Teillay* and *L'Elisabeth* off the coast of Cornwall by the Lizard. A fierce day long battle ensued between the two larger ships with neither able to gain the advantage. The 64 guns which both ships had wrought massive damage. Anthony Walsh steadfastedly refused the Prince's request that *du Teillay* should also join the battle. It was unthinkable that the Prince's own life should be placed at risk. *du Teillay* remained sheltered behind *L'Elisabeth* throughout the engagement.

The panel was embroidered by Elizabeth Duke and Lynne Schroder of Prestonpans. Liz's grandfather William Thomson was the last pilot for ships on the Forth out of Morrison's Haven so it was a bonus to be embroidering the Prince's L'Elisabeth. Lynne is an artist in many media and together they enjoyed creating their contribution to local history.

9th JULY

L'ELISABETH ENGAGES IN SEA BATTLE WITH ENGLISH LION

6 L'Elisabeth and HMS Lion are both so badly damaged they have no choice but to return to port – July 9th

Both *L' Elisabeth* and *HMS Lion* were so badly damaged by the end of the day that they had to break off the engagement. Captain L'Oe of *L' Elisabeth* and his brother both died in the action. More than 140 of the 700 soldiers aboard their ship were killed by the exchanges of fire, and many more were wounded. *L' Elisabeth* was fully dismasted and was listing so badly it was impossible to transfer any supplies, muskets, broadswords or the surviving French soldiers to *du Teillay*. *L' Elisabeth* limped back to Brest and took no further part in the campaign. *HMS Lion* was in no better condition and it too had to make its way back to Plymouth.

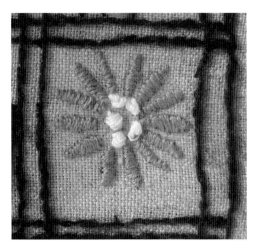

The panel was embroidered by Janet Goodall who has assisted with the embroidery of the Communion linen for Prestongrange Church – from whose tower some watched the battle in 1745. So she felt the wish to be involved. But travelling to France in Quercy she was able to engage their attention too during her language classes – and they are naturally keen to see the end result! Previous experience of embroidery has included the Pans' Mercat Cross and the Unicorn for a TOC H banner. Her tag records her keen interest in flower arranging.

panel 6

L'Elisabeth and HMS Lion are both so badly damaged they have no choice but to return to port – July 9th

7   du Teillay sails on alone to Scotland – July 9th – 23rd

After the disastrous loss of *L'Elisabeth*, the *du Teillay* sailed on alone to Scotland with the Prince and his immediate companions. There were now no supporting French soldiers. Their journey was further hindered by bad weather and the presence of English squadrons. One close encounter with the English occured on July 11th, but using the navigational skills of Duncan Cameron of Barra, and subsequently of Roderick McNeil's piper who came aboard at Barra on July 22nd, they escaped interception and arrived safely in the Outer Hebrides.

panel 7

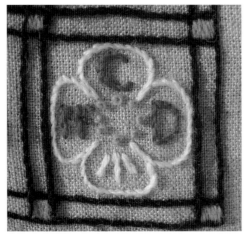

This panel was embroidered by Kate [Catharine] McDonald from Dalgety Bay whose ancestors were born at Kinlochmoidart with great great grandmother tending the light at Ardnamurchan Point 80 years after the Prince sailed those waters. Whilst teaching she joined the SWRI 'Rurals' and became an Evelyn Baxter scholar travelling around Scotland teaching beadwork in embroidery and jewellery. She's a member of the NTS needlework group based at Culross who are stitching a large crewel work panel for Falkland Palace. She learnt of the tapestry from a cutting a friend kept for her from *The Scotsman*.

9th JULY

DU TEILLAY SAILS ON TO SCOTLAND

8 du Teillay anchors at Eriskay and The Prince goes ashore in disguise – July 23rd

The Prince first came ashore, still in his disguise, on the small island of Eriskay in the Outer Hebrides on July 23rd 1745. As he walked on the strand some seeds which the Prince had earlier collected in France fell from his pocket onto the beach. Over the centuries they gave that strand a flower that is to this day known locally as Prince Charlie's Rose – a pink sea-bindweed flower with a white stripe whose botanical name is *calystegia soldanella*. The beach is always called The Prince's 'cockleshell' Strand in commemoration of his first landfall in Scotland.

This panel was quite properly stitched in the Hall on Eriskay by Sue MacDonald and Neilina MacInnes with the indispensable support of Helen MacLean, Christine Mitchell and Lena MacLellan who travelled over the Causeway from Uist each winter Thursday regardless of the weather – not for Whisky Galore but Earl Grey tea. 'We five got together after the BattleBus came to Eriskay in July 2009. In return for the embroidery tuition provided by the Uist Girls, we entertained them with the Eriskay news and our social calendar!!' [Just as it should be – Moran Taing Eriskay.]

23ʳᵈ JULY ☒ COILLEAG A'PHRIONNSA ☒ EIRISGEIDH ☒ ERISKAY ☒

PRINCE'S FLOWER

CALYSTEGIA SOLDANELLA

du TEILLAY ANCHORS AND THE PRINCE AS A PRIEST COMES ASHORE

panel 8

9 Alexander MacDonald advises against the campaign but the Prince is determined – July 24th

The Prince met first with local chief Alexander MacDonald of Boisdale who advised him that without French military support, which had been lost when *L'Elisabeth* had been forced to return to Brest, the campaign could not succeed.

Boisdale concluded: *"Go home".* Sir Thomas Sheridan and the Jacobite Duke of Atholl in the Prince's party both argued the

same. But the Prince was absolutely determined to press ahead, responding: *"I am come home Sir, and I will entertain no notion at all of returning to that place from whence I came; for that I am persuaded my faithful Highlanders will stand by me!"*

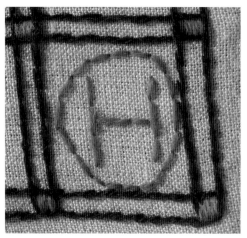

The panel was embroidered by Helen MacLean in the Outer Hebrides. Helen believes she's a selfish stitcher but couldn't resist the opportunity to take part in creating a national treasure and has enjoyed it tremendously. She's been knitting and stitching all her life and nobody can remember teaching her and she can't remember learning! Helen also stitched #11.

Alexander MacDonald advises against the campaign but the Prince is determined – July 24th

10 du Teillay carries the Prince to Arisaig and he stays at Borrodale House – July 25th / August 11th

After the Prince had spent his first night at Eriskay in a black house and his second back on board, the *du Teillay* sailed across to Loch nan Uamh. He landed, still in disguise as a student at the Scottish College in Paris, just east of Arisaig on July 25th. There he lodged with Angus MacDonald at Borrodale House. By now word was out that the Prince had arrived but Cameron of Lochiel was afraid to come to Borrodale lest he accede to the Prince's wishes and join the campaign. He sent his brother Dr Archibald Cameron to Borrodale to try to persuade the Prince to return to France. But the Prince remained adamant.

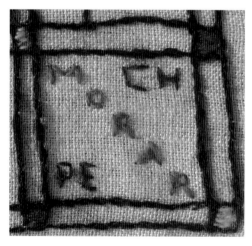

The panel was embroidered by Christine Haynes and Pauline Elwell who both stay in Morar close by its famous silver sands. Ann Lamont, editor of Westword, invited us to create a panel after a visit to Arisaig by the Battle Trustees in 2009. We have been greatly pleased by the whole experience and the end result.

25th JULY "COMA MUR AN TIG THU IDIR, MUR AN TIG THU NIS A CHLISGEADH:" MACDONALD

LOCH NAN UAMH

DU TEILLEY CARRIES THE PRINCE TO ARISAIG AND HE STAYS AT BORRODALE HOUSE

MO CH OR A PE AR

11   Letters are written to Clan Chiefs for their support

By now the Prince is convinced his campaign can succeed. Seated at Borrodale House he immediately writes and despatches letters to Clan Chiefs throughout the Highlands and on the east coast, seeking their support and informing them his Standard is to be raised at Glenfinnan. Messengers carried them swiftly across the Highlands and rumours abound.

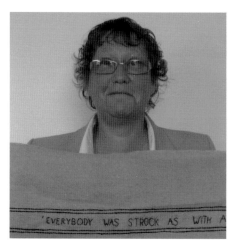

The panel was embroidered by Helen MacLean in the Outer Hebrides. Helen believes she's a selfish stitcher but couldn't resist the opportunity to take part in creating a national treasure and has enjoyed it tremendously. She's been knitting and stitching all her life and nobody can remember teaching her and she can't remember learning!

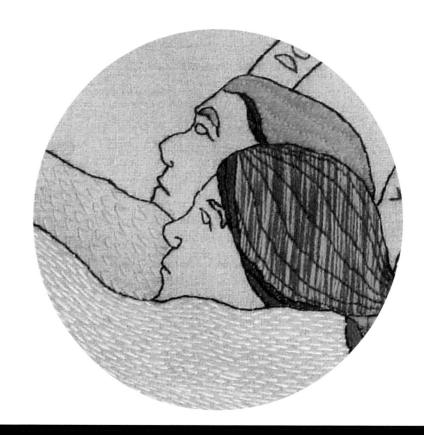

THE KING HAS LANDED

26th JULY

DONALD MacDONALD OF KINLOCHMOIDART

YOUNG CLANRANALD

ALEXANDER MacDONALD OF GLENALADALE

RANALD MacDONALD

LETTERS ARE WRITTEN TO CLAN CHIEFS ASKING FOR THEIR SUPPORT

12 Clanranald Warmly Welcome the Prince at Borrodale – July 26th

Despite the reluctance being shown in many quarters, Clanranald had no doubts that if the Prince was amongst them they must give all the aid they could. The whole neighbourhood at Arisaig without distinction of sex or age came to Borrodale to acknowledge him. Charles sat so he could be seen as they all ate together. The Prince gave a toast in English, which most could not understand but one present in responding translated the same toast into Gaelic – *"Deoch slaint an Righ!"* Hearing this the Prince asked that he repeat it so that he could make the toast again himself – which he did to everyone's delight.

The panel was started by Edith Smith of Musselburgh with its embroidery completed by Audrey Brown from North Berwick and Margaret Holm of Gullane. Edith is a member of Fibretrix – an artistic group of ladies who work experimentally in different textile mediums and who all played a part in the embroidery. Margaret and Audrey are both keen stitchers and were members of creative embroidery classes at North Berwick Community Centre.

13 Prince awaits responses to his letters

These are anxious days for the Prince. Will the Clan Chiefs, many of whom had made great sacrifices in 1715 often losing their lands and being forced into exile, respond to his appeal? He knows full well that he needs the support of Cameron of Lochiel and that if that can be achieved others will surely follow. The Chiefs' anxieties are heightened by the absence of any French support but there is nothing the Prince can do about that at this juncture. If the Clans rise with him, he assures them, *then* the French will come.

This panel was embroidered in Inversek by Ann Fraser [Scott-Kerr] who studied drawing and painting as a mature student at Edinburgh College of Art. Lady Ann's botanical painting has often been honoured by the Royal Horticultural Society. She read an article in East Lothian Life on the Prestonpans Tapestry and wanted to become involved because many of her ancestors were Jacobites. 'My family home was Sunlaws [now The Roxburghe Hotel] near Kelso where the Prince slept 4th/5th November en route to Carlisle and he planted a white rose tree'. Lady Ann's tag is appropriately The Jacobite Rose depicting not only her family's allegiance to the Jacobite cause but also her career as a botanical artist.

THE PRINCE AWAITS THE CLANS AT BORRODALE

'DON QUIKSOT'S EXPEDITION'

14   The Prince Orders du Teillay to depart – July 27th

Captain Walsh was reluctant to keep the *du Teillay* at anchor with many ships of the Royal Navy patrolling along the coast. He was therefore ready to leave and the Prince believed the ship's departure would act as a clear signal of his determination to pursue his campaign even though few positive responses had yet arrived to his letters to the Clan Chiefs. The *du Teillay's* crew unloaded 1500 muskets, 1800 broadswords, powder and small pieces of artillery and stored them in a nearby cave. That done, the *du Teillay* departed for France, privateering on its way home.

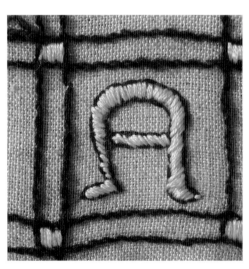

This panel was embroidered by Helen Brodie and Vera MacDonald of Arisaig, both of whom learned some needlework at school but had done little since. This and the second Arisaig panel #16 are the 'miracle' panels – having firstly been sent to Eriskay by mistake, then their Chief Stitcher left the village and finally another broke her wrist. It might not sound like fun but 'with a little help and an instruction book we were enthused and thoroughly enjoyed the experience'. The tag is the Celtic A for Arisaig.

27th JULY · 1500 MUSKETS, 1800 BROADSWORDS, POWDER AND SMALL FIELD PIECES.

PRINCE ORDERS THE DUTEILLAY TO UNLOAD & DEPART

panel 14

15   Lochiel comes to Borrodale – July 30th

Finally Cameron of Lochiel agrees to visit the Prince at Borrodale and, as he always feared he would be, is persuaded to give his pledge that his Camerons will rally to his Standard when it is raised. Lochiel insists, however, on one condition.

MacDonald of Glengarry must come out with the Prince too. To the Prince's delight, Glengarry agrees he will. All is now set for the Standard to be raised at Glenfinnan and the date is confirmed.

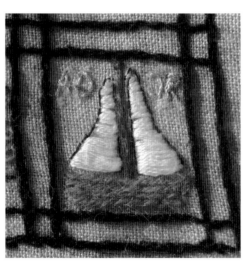

panel 15

This panel was embroidered in East Lothian by Janet Raeburn and Alison Dickson, who she recruited to help. They wanted to be part of what they saw as a 'huge' undertaking having read about its progress in *East Lothian Life*. It was fun from start to finish with visits to the Cockenzie Studio of Andrew Crummy three times when challenges needed third opinions. "Alas, it is finished!"

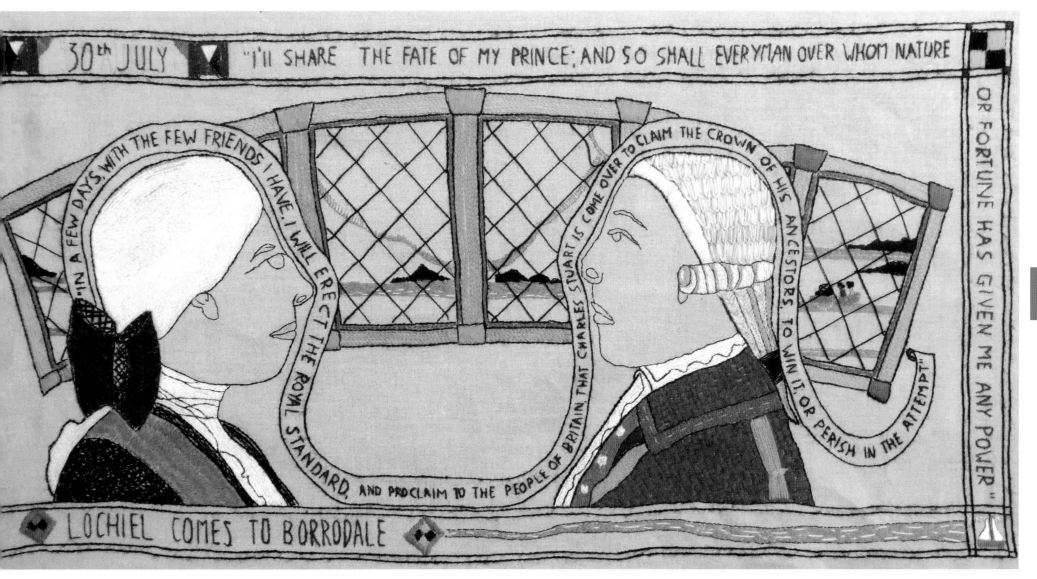

16 The Prince crosses to Kinlochmoidart House – August 11th / 17th

On August 11th the Prince travelled by sea to Kinlochmoidart House, home of Donald MacDonald of Moidart. He travelled with the artillery taken from *du Teillay* and the baggage. His bodyguard from the Clanranalds marched by the shore. It was here he waited whilst final preparations were made for Glenfinnan. Whilst staying with Donald MacDonald the Prince received further promises of support and was joined briefly by John Maclean of Mull.

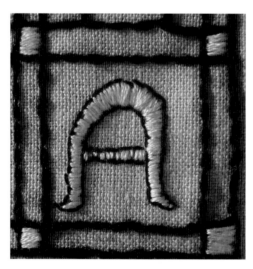

panel 16

This panel was embroidered by Anne Cameron, June Cairns and Rose MacEachen, all of whom had learned some needlework at school. June has attended several schools and classes run by the SWRI as a Member, but frankly had not practised much between times. 'All the Arisaig Stitchers, here and for #14, relied on Ruth Smither before she left the village for guidance and much of the needlework. 'However, once started our confidence grew and we feel so proud of what we have managed that we are looking for our next project to work on.'

11th – 17th AUGUST

ARISAIG
BORRODALE
LOCH NAN UAMH
LOCH AILORT
GLENUIG BAY
FORSAY
MOIDART
KINLOCHMOIDART HOUSE
HOME OF DONALD MACDONALD
DALILEA
LOCH SHIEL
GLENALADALE
GLENFINNAN

MOIDART SEVEN SIGN A BOND

◆ THE PRINCE ARRIVES AT KINLOCHMOIDART HOUSE ◆

17   John Murray of Broughton joins the Prince at Kinlochmoidart – August 17th

The Prince's last day at Kinlochmoidart House is made that much more enjoyable by the arrival of John Murray of Broughton, a long standing friend from Rome and France. He becomes The Prince's Secretary of State throughout the campaign. [However, John Murray's name and reputation are forever sullied in 1746 when he turns King's Evidence to George II after his own imprisonment in London and betrays several leading Jacobite supporters – most particularly Lord Lovat who is tried before the bar of the House of Lords and executed.]

This panel was embroidered by a group from Kinlochmoidart on Loch Moidart led by Helen Nairn. They included Nino Stewart, to whom the House is home today, Marjorie Watters, Heather Cochrane, Frances Maclean and Debbie Muir. Although each had some sewing experience such embroidery was a new challenge for them all working round the clock to complete the panel in eight weeks. 'We enjoyed working on the panel and everyone of us felt that it was very fitting indeed that it was being stitched and completed here on the Kinlochmoidart estate'.

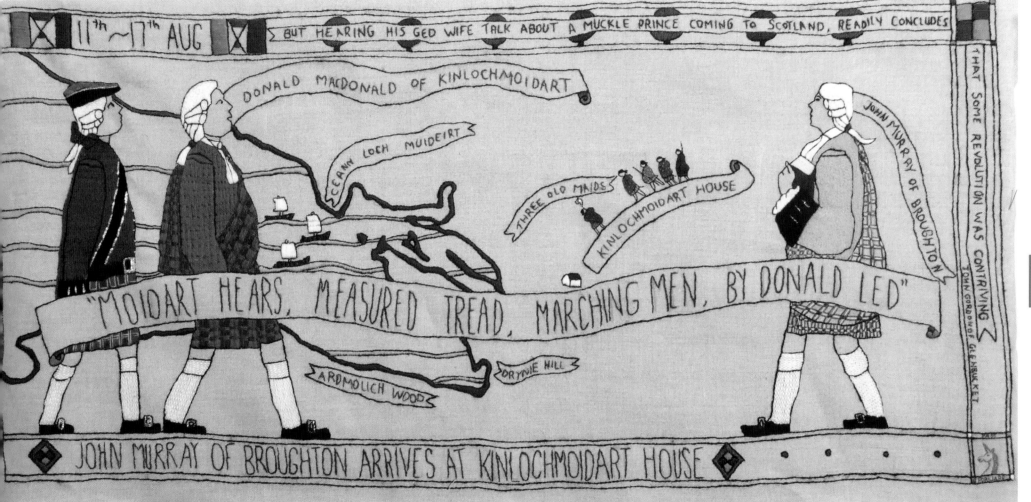

11th ~ 17th AUG

BUT HEARING HIS GED WIFE TALK ABOUT A MUCKLE PRINCE COMING TO SCOTLAND, READILY CONCLUDES

DONALD MACDONALD OF KINLOCHMOIDART

CEANN LOCH MUIDEIRT

THREE OLD MAIDS

KINLOCHMOIDART HOUSE

JOHN MURRAY OF BROUGHTON

THAT SOME REVOLUTION WAS CONTRIVING

JOHN GORDON OF GLENBUCKET

"MOIDART HEARS, MEASURED TREAD, MARCHING MEN, BY DONALD LED"

ARDMOLICH WOOD

DRYNIE HILL

JOHN MURRAY OF BROUGHTON ARRIVES AT KINLOCHMOIDART HOUSE

18   The Seven Men of Moidart are recognised

The Prince's immediate companions who had crossed from France, and travelled across from Borrodale on August 11th to Kinlochmoidart, continued to accompany him throughout these anxious times. It was from this moment that they became known to history as 'The Seven Men of Moidart'. Only two were Scots; one was English and the remaining four were Irish. [They are commemorated today at Kinlochmoidart by seven beech trees.]

The panel was embroidered by Elma Colvin who normally works with silk and dyes designing large wall hangings – often a solitary experience. Embroidering this panel was totally new and exciting for me – the scale of it all, the organisation and research involved, working with so many others and learning a great deal more personally about the Battle of Prestonpans. "Working together has its own creative magic – and it's fun!"

SIR JOHN MACDONALD
SIR THOMAS SHERIDAN
COLONEL FRANCIS STRICKLAND
JOHN WILLIAM O'SULLIVAN
GEORGE KELLY
WILLIAM MARQUIS OF TULLIBARDINE
DUKE OF ATHOLL
AENEAS MACDONALD

THE SEVEN MEN OF MOIDART

19 Sir John Cope organises the baking of bread in Edinburgh – August 16th

Sir John Cope, Commander-in-Chief in Scotland of the Hanoverian government army, the redcoats, had learnt of the Prince's landing from spies in the Highlands. He made careful preparations to march from Edinburgh for Stirling, and from there to Fort William via the Corrieyairack Pass. However, he knew the Highlands would be hostile and in any event anticipated very considerable difficulties in obtaining supplies as he marched. So he wisely insisted that the bakers of Leith, Edinburgh and Stirling prepare bread as biscuit to carry on his expedition. Its preparation delayed the redcoats march north from Stirling by more than a day which was to prove crucial in his attempt to cross the Corrieyairack Pass.

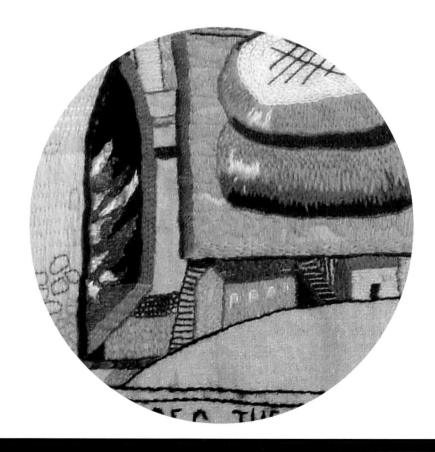

The panel was embroidered by Dorie Wilkie of Eskbank, the 'earliest' volunteer who became Lead Stitcher for the tapestry. After raising her family she took City & Guilds in Embroidery then worked at Leith School of Art. She is currently Secretary of the Costume Society of Scotland. Her tag was inspired by the stone plaque above the main door of Argyle's Lodging in Stirling [and her named family in support].

16ᵗʰ AUGUST

COPE ORGANISES THE BAKING OF THE BREAD IN EDINBURGH

20 Donald MacDonnell of Tirnadris captures redcoats at High Bridge in the first skirmish of the campaign – August 16th

Sir John Cope had already ordered 90 men from the 1st Royal Regiment of Foot to march from Perth to reinforce the garrison at Fort William. They made good progress to Fort Augustus and on August 16th embarked on the final 25 miles to Fort William. Knowing of their march, Alexander MacDonnell of Keppoch sent his cousin, Donald MacDonnell of Tirnadris, with just eleven men and a piper, to intercept them at the inn at the south end of the High Bridge across the River Spean, whilst Keppoch himself gathered sufficient clan members to oppose the redcoats. However, before they could arrive the redcoats reached the High Bridge. Tirnadris commanded his piper to play and his eleven men proceeded to trick the redcoat commander into believing they faced a much larger force. After a brief skirmish, the first of the campaign, in which six redcoats were killed, the redcoats withdrew. Tirnadris continued to harrass them until Keppoch arrived supported by a party of Glengarrys and the redcoats finally surrendered.

The panel was embroidered by Hilary Williams, a Poldrate Quilter staying in Gullane although she's from well south of the border. Born and brought up in Lancashire she lived in Hampshire and Dorset before travelling across the world to stay in Hawaii there to learn her sewing skills. Stitching the tapestry has been a 'wonderful' new experience for Hilary both gaining understanding of the Prince's story and sharing the creation of her panel with artist Andrew Crummy and fellow stitchers.

16TH AUGUST

RIVER SPEAN

DONALD MACDONNELL OF TIRNADRIS LEADS CAPTURE OF REDCOATS AFTER ACTION AT HIGHBRIDGE

Donald MacDonnell of Tirnadris captures redcoats at High Bridge in the first skirmish of the campaign – August 16th

21 Galley Boats depart from Dalilea Pier for Glenaladale on Loch Shiel – August 18th

After receiving sufficient assurances of support for the raising of the Standard at Glenfinnan the Prince was ready to make his way there. Accordingly, on August 18th he began the journey up Loch Shiel in galley boats departing from the pier at Dalilea. He was accompanied by some 50 from Clanranald as his bodyguard as well as by his 'Seven Men of Moidart'. Dalilea House was home to the distinguished Gaelic poet Alasdair MacMaighsteir, Bard of Clanranald, who joined the Prince as his Gaelic tutor and T*yrtaeus* [elegiac poet].

En route the Prince and his followers stayed the night at Glenaladale House with Alexander MacDonald and were joined from Aberdeenshire by John Gordon of Glenbucket and a captured government officer, Captain Sweetenham of Guise's 6th Foot, who had been en route from Ruthven Barracks to Fort William to take command and reinforce that garrison. He had been taken without a fight by a party of Glengarry Kennedys on August 14th as he crested the Corrieyairack Pass along with some sixty soldiers.

The panel was embroidered by Jean Dawson originally from Northumberland but longtime stayer in Gullane. She is pictured stitching on her 70th birthday whilst away on family holiday in Norfolk with Fiona, Simon, Stewart, Claire and grandchildren Angus and Olivia. 'I enjoyed embroidery in my teens but for many years couldn't find the time whilst bringing up family and playing tennis, squash, badminton and golf. But I recently started learning furniture upholstering and it was during one of those classes that it was suggested I sign up for a panel. It has been therapeutic. I was diagnosed last year with angina and underwent surgery so sitting quietly at embroidery has been a great help to my recovery. The panel is already very well travelled as I spend a lot of time 'dog and house' sitting and it always accompanied me'.

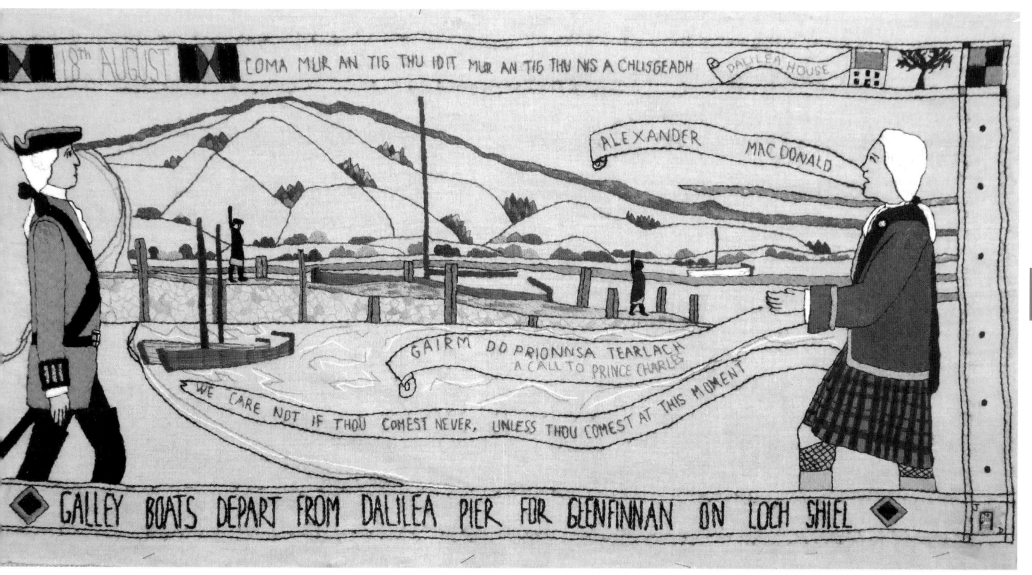

18TH AUGUST COMA MUR AN TIG THU IDIT MUR AN TIG THU NIS A CHUISGEADH DALILEA HOUSE

ALEXANDER MACDONALD

GAIRM DO PRIONNSA TEARLACH
A CALL TO PRINCE CHARLES

WE CARE NOT IF THOU COMEST NEVER, UNLESS THOU COMEST AT THIS MOMENT

GALLEY BOATS DEPART FROM DALILEA PIER FOR GLENFINNAN ON LOCH SHIEL

Galley Boats depart from Dalilea Pier for Glenaladale on Loch Shiel – August 18th

22 Galley Boats arrive from Glenaladale at Glenfinnan and the Prince awaits the clans – August 19th

The Prince made the second stage of his journey up Loch Sheil from Glenaladale at Glenfinnan, departing at 7 am on the morning of August 19th. He arrived before noon hoping to receive a rapturous and tumultous welcome, but the shore was silent. By one o'clock, the time appointed for the rendez-vous, only an additional 350 Clanranald MacDonalds of Morar had arrived. The Prince waited impatiently in a shepherd's hut. Would Lochiel honour his pledge and come to see the Standard raised?

This panel was embroidered by Kate [Catharine] McDonald from Dalgety Bay whose ancestors were born at Kinlochmoidart with great great grandmother tending the light at Ardnamurchan Point 80 years after the Prince sailed those waters. Whilst teaching she joined the SWRI 'Rurals' and became an Evelyn Baxter scholar travelling around Scotland teaching beadwork in embroidery and jewellery. She's a member of the NTS needlework group based at Culross who are stitching a large crewel work panel for Falkland Palace. She learnt of the tapestry from a cutting a friend kept for her from *The Scotsman*.

19th AUGUST

GALLEY BOATS ARRIVE FROM GLENALADALE AT GLENFINNAN

23 Sir John Cope leaves Edinburgh heading for Fort William – August 19th

Sir John Cope marches from Stirling into the Highlands in the hope he can reach Fort William and cut off the Prince's campaign. He reached Crieff on 20th with five companies of Lee's and Murray's Regiments and two of Lord John Murray's Highlanders. There he was joined by eight more companies of Lascelles' Regiment. Thus reinforced, he proceeded swiftly to Amulree on 22nd, Taybridge on 23rd, Trinifuir on 24th and

Dalnacardoch on 25th. Gardiner's dragoons had deliberately remained behind at Stirling to defend the Forth, with Hamilton's left in Edinburgh to defend the capital. The dragoons were in any event of limited military value in the Highlands and cannons were difficult to transport despite the roads Marshal Wade had built after the 1715 Jacobite uprising.

The panel was embroidered by Yvonne Murphy of Port Seton, who came to the community from South Africa in 1998. In 2006 she became a Founding Member of the 3Harbours Festival and enjoys the hive of artistic activity across the area. 'I thought I was too busy to be able to embroider my panel but seeing the excitement and exquisite work emerging I was soon taking home my linen. I've had enormous help from fellow artists and took my embroidery, with more than one other, to the Boatie Blest camp at Portsoy. Now I look forward to recovering from embroiderers' neck!' Yvonne's tag colours recall her origins in South Africa, the seagulls that visit her garden and the boat her new/ next life in Scotland.

19th AUG

"THAT PROVIDING BREAD HAS BEEN THE ONLY STOP TO THE TROOPS MARCHING" COPE

STIRLING CASTLE

FIRTH OF FORTH

EDINBURGH CASTLE

SIR COPE LEAVES EDINBURGH HEADING FOR FORT WILLIAM

Sir John Cope leaves Edinburgh heading for Fort William – August 19th

24   Cameron of Lochiel arrives at Glenfinnan – August 19th

Finally by 4 pm at Glenfinnan the skirling of the pipes could be heard up the glen and Cameron of Lochiel appeared with more than seven hundred men zigzagging down the mountain path. His promise had been honoured. Lochiel was soon joined by MacDonnell of Keppoch with three hundred of his clansmen and by the late afternoon some 1200 clansmen were assembled at the head of the glen and on the surrounding hills. The Prince was exultant.

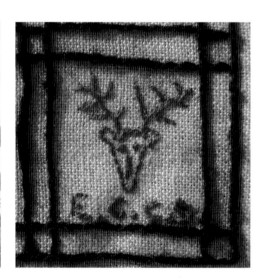

The panel was embroidered by Esther Sharpley whose love of the Highlands that rose for the Prince knows no bounds. She has walked in all seasons those very lands across which the Prince travelled – not least those of Cameron of Lochiel. To stitch this panel was especially rewarding as well as the links with so many other embroiderers across Scotland. Her tag is the Stag's head of her Clan MacKenzie.

"NEVER HAVE I SEEN ANYTHING SO QUAINTLY PLEASING AS THE MARCH OF THIS TROOP OF HIGHLANDERS AS THEY DESCENDED A STEEP

DONALD CAMERON OF LOCHIEL

MOUNTAINSIDE BY A ZIGZAG PATH SIR JOHN MACDONALD

LOCHIEL ARRIVES AT GLENFINNAN

25   The Prince's Standard is Raised by the Jacobite Duke of Atholl – August 19th

With the support of two men at his side the Jacobite Duke of Atholl carried the new Jacobite Standard, furled, across the River Finnan to the sound of the pipes. Next the Standard was blessed by Bishop Hugh MacDonald. Finally, on the command of the Prince the Standard of white and red was unfurled and held aloft to roars of approval. The Royal Commission from

King James VIII and III appointing Prince Charles as Regent was then read aloud followed by a Manifesto promising to dissolve the Union. The excitement was enormous, Lochiel for the moment setting his concerns aside. The Prince was totally elated although, perforce, he spent the night humbly in a small barn.

The panel was embroidered [l/r] by Sandra Casey, Sandra Provan and Ruth Casey of Fort William. Sandra Provan created the intricate main figures on the tapestry whilst Sandra Casey and daughter Rachel complemented her by stitching the outline and lettering. The panel has been enhanced by the personal support of Donald, Cameron of Lochiel, who hosted a number of stitchers from Lochaber at his ancestral home at Achnacarry. He gave them all great insight and guidance on the history of the '45 and enhancing details of Jenny Cameron and the colour of some of the banners.

The Prince's Standard is Raised by the Jacobite Duke of Atholl – August 19th

26   Lord Tweeddale Offers a reward of £30,000 for seizing the Prince – August 19th

When word reached Sir John Cope that the Prince had landed he made immediate preparations to leave for the Highlands. Lord Tweeddale, Secretary for North Britain in the Hanoverian government in London, who lived at Pinkie House, Musselburgh, shared in the planning and agreed what best should be done. Lord Tweeddale also announced a reward of £30,000 for anyone seizing the Prince, news of which reached him after he had left Glenfinnan. £30,000 was an immense sum that could have transformed the life of any claimant but it was never in prospect such was the fierce loyalty of the clans in support of the Prince.

The panel was embroidered by Dianne Laing of Innerwick, who has been involved with the archaeological digs at Prestongrange for the past five years and latterly at the battle site. With embroidery friend Shona MacManus [# 53] already involved she volunteered to stitch. It's been a most considerable learning curve with previous experience mainly addressing school buttons and using an electric machine. Time had to be found around her day job as a Fundraiser for Scottish Native Woods – 'but what an experience to share in such a lasting legacy!'

Lord Tweeddale Offers a reward of £30,000 for seizing the Prince – August 19th

27 The Prince Offers a Reward of £30,000 for the Elector of Hanover – August 25th

The Prince, hearing for the first time at Kinlochiel that a reward had been offered for his seizure, responded on August 25th with an equal offer for anyone seizing the Elector of Hanover, King George II. Initially Charles had jokingly suggested offering a derisory sum as a reward to make light of the Elector's value, but he was persuaded that others might misunderstand his humour. The £30,000 offer was matched.

The panel was embroidered by Maud Crawford of Dunblane who spent her childhood on the North Yorkshire Moors and the Isle of Mull. She leads a group of crewel embroiderers meeting throughout central Scotland. In sewing this panel her most difficult challenge was working out how to sew the wig with inspiration eventually coming from the drawing of Adam Smith from the 'Dear Economist' column in Weekend Financial Times. The tag on this panel is common to all seven stitched by the team in Dunblane and represents their fine Cathedral.

The Prince Offers a Reward of £30,000 for the Elector of Hanover – August 25th

28 The Prince Stays overnight at Fassfern and picks a white rose – August 23rd/24th

The Prince's stay overnight at Fassfern saw John Cameron, Lochiel's brother and Fassfern's owner, deliberately absent. When the Prince arose next morning outside his bedroom window he saw the most beautiful white roses, one of which he picked and placed in his bonnet. Seeing him do this, the clansmen with him found many more white roses in the gardens and did likewise. Henceforth throughout the campaign the white rose, or white cockade, was to be the emblem of support for the Prince. Continuing their march, the Highlanders moved across the High Bridge and on to Laggan where Donald MacDonnell of Lochgarry joined with another 400 clansmen.

 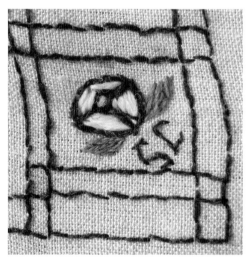

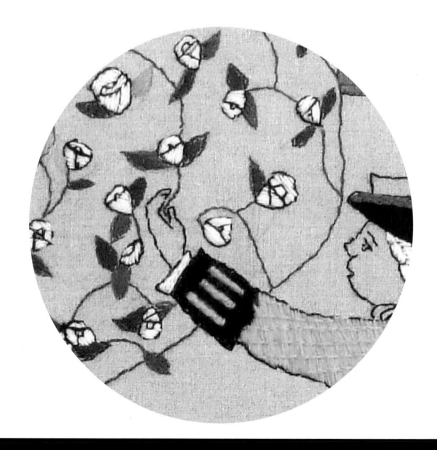

The panel was embroidered by Simone Cunningham, a Panner born and bred and sister to Faith-Ann Mulgrew [#102]. 'A mother of three and grandmother of two, I do voluntary work in the Pans community as a Guider in the 2nd Prestonpans Rainbows – which I started up in January 1995. I resolved to join in this embroidery project as I had been very interested in watching the annual re-enactments of the Battle. I have thoroughly enjoyed stitching my panel and feel that it is a great honour to be part of history.'

23RD–24TH AUGUST

THE PRINCE STAYS OVERNIGHT AT FASSFERN AND PICKS THE WHITE ROSE

29 The Highlanders by-pass Fort William – August 25th

Fort William had a small permanent garrison, depleted by the wars on the contient, which stood at the foot of the Great Glen close by Ben Nevis. Cope's two earlier initiatives from Perth and Ruthven to reinforce Fort William had failed but he still hoped to reach it himself via the Corrieyairack Pass to bar the Prince's way. The Prince was thinking well ahead of such a strategy, however, and was determined to spend no time attempting to lay siege to the Fort. The Highlanders passed to the north proceeding as swiftly as was possible.

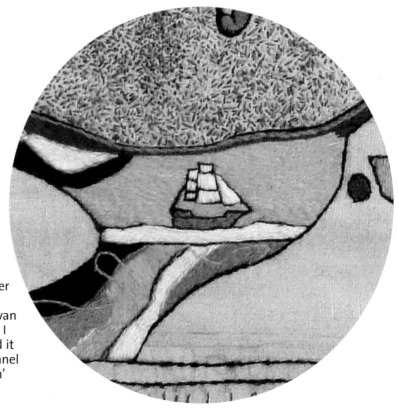

This panel was created by Margaret McCabe, daughter to Sarah [#80] and William – who stitched the naval boat! A proud Panner, Margaret [whose tag is a simple daisy surrounded by colours reminding her of her ever watchful cat Simba] lives just opposite the town's lucky charm, Johnnie Moat and her passionate vocation is child care. As an only child she learnt to occupy her time especially on wet caravan holidays with colouring books. 'I've dabbled in arts and crafts but never attempted embroidery before. I liken my panel to the most challenging colouring-in exercise I've ever embarked upon! And I've tackled it whilst also joining the Boatie Blest rowing crews stitching whilst on shore!' Margaret dedicates this panel to her grandparents James & Margaret Connachan who left their own legacy on industrious 'Priestoun' and to great grandfather John, the old grinder who played his button box in The Goth!

25TH AUGUST "TO CROSSE A CURSED MONTAIGNE, WHERE THE HORSES COULD HARDLY PASSE"

GLEN LOY

LOY

LOCH LOCHY

DRUIM FADA

RIVER LOCHY

LOCHIEL

FASSFERN

LOCH EIL

FORT WILLIAM

30 The Prince stays overnight at Invergarry Castle – August 26th

After passing through Laggan the Highlanders reached Invergarry Castle in pouring rains on August 26th, standing just short of the entrance to the Corrieyairack Pass. The Prince stayed overnight with MacDonnell of Glengarry whose clan provided some 600 Highlanders for the campaign. The MacDonnells had already been involved in the first successful action of the rising ten days before at High Bridge when 90 of Cope's intended redcoat reinforcements for Fort William had been captured [see Panel # 20].

This panel was created by Avril Wills, Lady of Prestoungrange in Prestonpans. It was her first major work of embroidery but one she could not miss having been involved as a Trustee of the Battle Heritage Trust since its foundation in 2006. She had also enjoyed 'signing off' visits across the Highlands in summer 2009 both in Eriskay and during the tapestry residency at Borrodale. Ann Fraser most kindly assisted.

26TH AUGUST

HIGHLANDERS MARCH THROUGH HEAVY RAIN TO INVERGARRY CASTLE

The Prince stays overnight at Invergarry Castle – August 26th

31 The Highlanders skirt Fort Augustus and reach the Corrieyairack Pass – August 27th

At Invergarry Castle on August 26th the Prince was immediately joined by 260 Stewarts of Appin led by Ardshiel. Intelligence reports suggested that Sir John Cope was now at Dalwhinnie and preparing to march over the Corrieyairack Pass – the vital strategic choke point for the entire campaign here in the Highlands. Overnight, Glengarry MacDonald's clansmen, MacDonald of Glencoe and some Grants of Glenmoriston at Aberchalder also joined the Prince. As earlier with Fort William on August 25th [Panel # 29], the Prince was determined to ignore Fort Augustus to avoid any delays. Accordingly the Highlanders arrived at the foot of the Corrieyairack Pass on August 27th ready to cross first.

The panel was embroidered by Laurence Le Quéré who was born and brought up in Normandy near Rouen. As au-pair in the UK she met husband Simon Boxall and ended up staying for nine years. Now back in France for twelve years they live in Angoulême, loves sewing and is self-taught. She enjoyed doing her panel so much she took it with her everywhere, to the beach, camping and in the car whilst travelling or waiting for her son Ben to finish judo.

The Highlanders skirt Fort Augustus and reach the Corrieyairack Pass – August 27th

32 Sir John Cope reaches Dalwhinnie and his officers vote to proceed to Inverness – August 27th

When Cope arrived at Dalwhinnie on August 26th he was wrongly led to believe the Highlanders *already held* the Corrieyairack Pass and were waiting to ambush him there. If such an ambush occured it would have been disastrous in the light of alarmist reports from scouting parties suggesting the Prince's army had grown to 3,800 with more than 24 cannons. Cope held a crucial meeting of all his officers and on the 27th they unanimously resolved to abandon plans to cross the Corrieyairack Pass. Instead they would proceed directly to Inverness, Cope taking the precaution of getting all his officers literally to 'sign up' for the decision. By heading to Inverness Cope left the way open for the Prince to proceed directly towards Edinburgh without hindrance. Cope reached Ruthven later on August 27th and marched from there to Dalrachny on 28th.

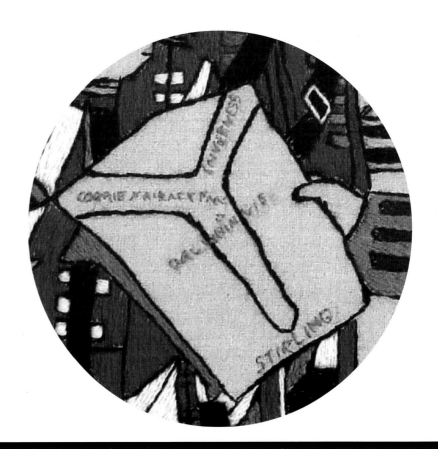

The panel was embroidered by Christina Russell who is a member of the Dunbar Castle Quilters and the SWRI Rurals – where she has leant many crafts over the past 40 years. Born in Perth she was educated at Bridge of Earn before coming to East Lothian when she was 11.

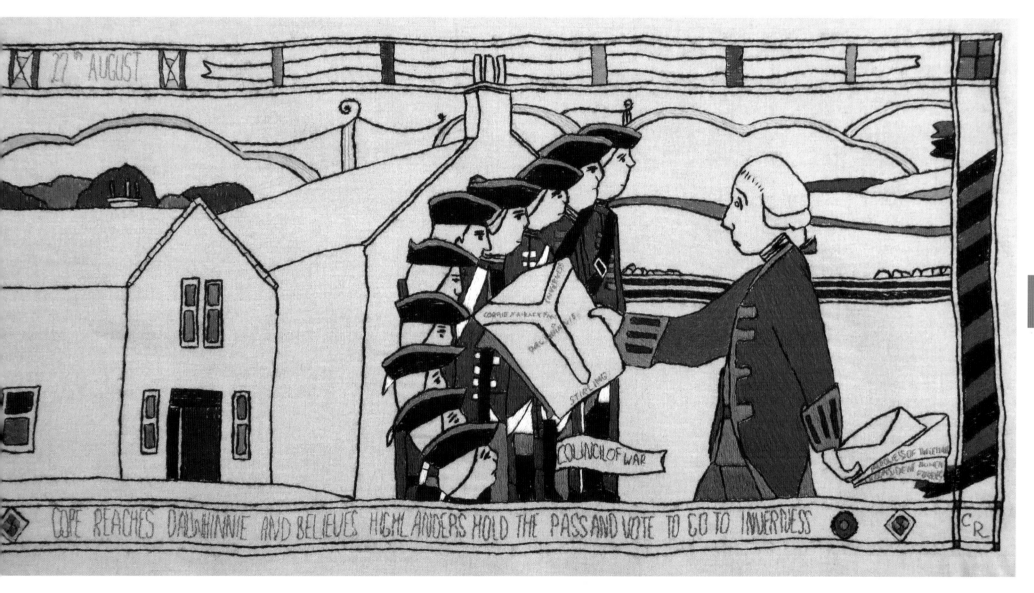

COPE REACHES DALWHINNIE AND BELIEVES HIGHLANDERS HOLD THE PASS AND VOTE TO GO TO INVERNESS

33 The Highlanders cross the Corrieyairack Pass – August 28th

The Highlanders had not beaten Cope to the Corrieyairack Pass. There was no ambush. But with Cope deceived the redcoats had missed their chance by proceeding on to Inverness. The Highlanders did finally cross the Corrieyairack on August 28th, arriving at Garvemore to the east and very much hoping to find Cope and do battle. But it was not to be. At an urgent Council of War it was initially proposed to head through Strathdearn to intercept Cope at Sliochmuick, but it was eventually decided he was too far ahead. A party of Camerons did however seize Ewen MacPherson of Cluny who had supported Cope but who readily changed his allegiance. The following day the Highlanders made their way to Dalwhinnie and from thence to Dalnacardoch.

panel 33

The panel was embroidered by Katherine Shaw of Edinburgh, a lifelong teacher of Home Economics in schools and with adults, with City & Guilds in Embroidery. 'I've loved the drop-in sessions and although I live by the Pentland Hills it is so nice to be by the sea with your friendly welcome and seeing the other panels progressing. Stitching along the drawn lines seemed never ending but then I did the bonnets and one kilt and like magic the picture came alive. Stitching allows me to be still, frees yet challenges my mind and is immensely satisfying. I dedicate my panel to James, Barbara, Chris, Charlie, Judith, Martin, Ross and Lynda and my tag is wee grandson Charlie, on the tractor at that favourite – Gorgie City Farm.

28 AUGUST FORT AUGUSTUS MELGARVE GARVA BRIDGE LAGGAN BRIDGE

GENERAL GEORGE WADE

HIGHLANDERS CROSS THE CORRIEYAIRACK PASS

34 Redcoats pursued to Ruthven Barracks but Highlanders repulsed by Sargeant Molloy – August 29th

Whilst the main body of Highlanders had continued towards Dalwhinnie some 90 Highlanders under O'Sullivan and Dr Archibald Cameron attacked the Ruthven Barracks nearby. They were lightly garrisoned by redcoat Sargeant Molloy with but twelve men. The Highlanders hoped to capture some of Cope's supplies left there as he had marched swiftly north. However, the Jacobites lacked any artillery and Ruthven was a very well protected fort. Molloy repulsed the attack inflicting two deaths and several more casualties and the attempt was quickly abandoned.

panel 34

The panel was embroidered by Elizabeth Jones of Prestonpans who also completed Panel # 72 setting down the Battle Lines on September 21st. "I've enjoyed every stitch, such a great project to be involved with and I hope it brings pleasure to everyone who views it in the years to come. For its creation, so many talented people have been brought together by a strand of wool to tell our nation's history."

Redcoats pursued to Ruthven Barracks but Highlanders repulsed by Sargeant Molloy – August 29th

35   Sir John Cope arrives at Inverness – August 29th

Cope arrived at Inverness on August 29th and reinforced the garrison there, remaining in the town until September 4th. He sent orders to Edinburgh for shipping to be sent to Aberdeen so that he could transport his army to the Firth of Forth ports, which decision was speedily notified to the Highlanders. The Prince immediately convened a Council of War which considered seeking to intercept Cope between Inverness and Aberdeen but again resolved to march south as swiftly as possible to take Edinburgh before Cope could get back there by sea. Meanwhile the Elector of Hanover, King George II, arrived back in London from Hanover on August 31st.

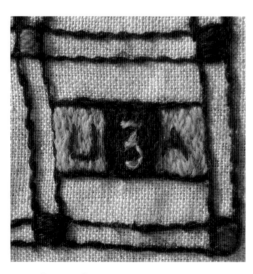

The panel was embroidered by Joan Campbell [seated] and left to right Hazel Bennett, May Bowie [leader], Margaret Hogg & Barbara Armstrong. They're all members of the University of the Third Age [U3A] in the Craft/Cross Stitch Set of East Lothian who share and enjoy this and many other leisure and learning interests.

36 The Prince stays at Blair Castle – August 31st – September 3rd

The Prince's hosts at Blair Castle, which was in the process of being extended at the time, were William the Jacobite Duke of Atholl and William's widowed cousin, Lady Lude. Lord George Murray, William's brother, was in Perth at the time trying to raise more men for the cause. Despite the necessity of reaching Edinburgh as soon as possible, the Prince urgently needed to gather fresh supplies and funds for his campaign. Whilst he waited at Blair Castle he tasted fresh pineapple for the first time and was introduced to the game of bowls. He and his followers enjoyed a ball organised by Lady Lude who was so delighted by it all that she was described as behaving 'like a light giglet.' The Prince was joined by John Roy Stewart and a number of local Jacobite lairds and the important Atholl Brigade was reconstituted. [Blair Castle today has, among its many treasures, Jacobite items belonging to the Prince and Lord George Murray.]

The panel was embroidered by members of Clan Donnachaidh – Robertsons all, led by Sylvia of that latter name. They are members of the Rannoch and Highland Branch. Pictured l/r Jenny Stark, Ginnie Wilkie, Sylvia and Ann McBay. Other helpers, aged 4 – bus pass +, were Betty, Ingrid and Seonag Robertsons and Jean Cameron with Iris and Flora Stark. Chatting and laughter were the order of the day when they came together from Perthshire, Caithness, Aberdeenshire and Germany to get their stitching done. Lady Lude's gown is decorated with violets for faithfulness, and primroses for youth and the hope they bring for new beginnings.

31st AUGUST ~ 3rd SEPTEMBER   LORD GEORGE MURRAY

DUKE WILLIAM   LADY LUDE   LIKE A LIGHT GIGLET

THE PRINCE STAYS AT BLAIR CASTLE

37 The Prince arrives in Perth and is joined by Lord George Murray – September 4th – 10th

Cameron of Lochiel had gone ahead and occupied Perth whilst the Prince rested at Blair Castle. On September 3rd the Prince followed, marching through the Pass of Killiecrankie to Dunkeld and arriving in triumphal procession in Perth on the evening of September 4th. He set up his headquarters in the Salutation Inn personally staying at Lord Stormont's home nearby. One most welcome visitor was Colonel Bower of Kincaldrum whom the Prince saluted outside the Inn [giving it its name. That public greeting was later to be used in evidence against the Colonel in his trial in York as a Jacobite.] During the week the Prince busied himself raising taxes and seeking additional troops. Oliphant of Gask joined him as did the Earl of Airlie. Viscount Strathallan came with some cavalry and James Drummond, Duke of Perth, also volunteered. Most significantly of all, Lord George Murray, a 50 year old man and younger brother of the Duke of Atholl with considerable military experience lately in support of King George II, now joined the Prince. Murray was immediately appointed Lieutenant General and Deputy Commander of the Highland army. The Duke of Perth was given a similar rank.

This panel was embroidered by Jacquie McNally, who grew up in Perth but now lives in Musselburgh. Her parents, Alan and Irene Melville, first met, held their wedding reception, then Ruby Anniversary celebrations all in the very Salutation Inn depicted. Jacquie graduated in Printed Textile Design from Duncan Of Jordanstone College of Art followed by a short spell at Perth Theatre. After moving to London and the wardrobe department of the BBC, she then worked for a costume house, making costumes for theatre, film and television, eventually working at the Royal Opera House before returning to Scotland when son Charlie arrived in 2002.

Text within image:
4th SEPTEMBER — SCONE — LORD GEORGE MURRAY — DUKE OF PERTH — LORD STRATHALLAN — OLIPHANT OF GASK — EARL OF AIRLIE — RAISING TAXES

THE PRINCE ARRIVES IN PERTH AND GREETS COLONEL BOWER OF KINCALDRUM AT THE SALUTATION INN

38 Sir John Cope makes a forced march to Aberdeen – September 4th – 11th

Cope realised as soon as he left Dalwhinnie that he had to return as swiftly as possible to the Lowlands if he was to save Edinburgh. He left Inverness on September 4th reaching Aberdeen on the 11th. The 'forced' march took him through Nairn, Elgin, Fochabers, Cullen, Banff, Turriff and Old Meldrum.

Throughout this march, as had occured ever since he left Stirling, his Highlander Companies suffered desertions. Furthermore Cope was not joined by loyal Hanoverian Highland supporters as he had been led to believe he would.

The panel was embroidered by Jennifer Haldane of Dunblane. Her earliest memory was stitching together off cuts while her mother made their clothes, blanket stitching the edges and making needle cases. "I did dress making for GCSE and a foundation course of pattern cutting at Art College, making silk ties and selling them outside college". She made all the family's wedding clothes for her four children. She has been a member of the Embroiders Guild in Perth and learnt crewel work with the Dunblane group. "I am very proud to be part of such an enthusiastic project and am longing to see all the finished panels".

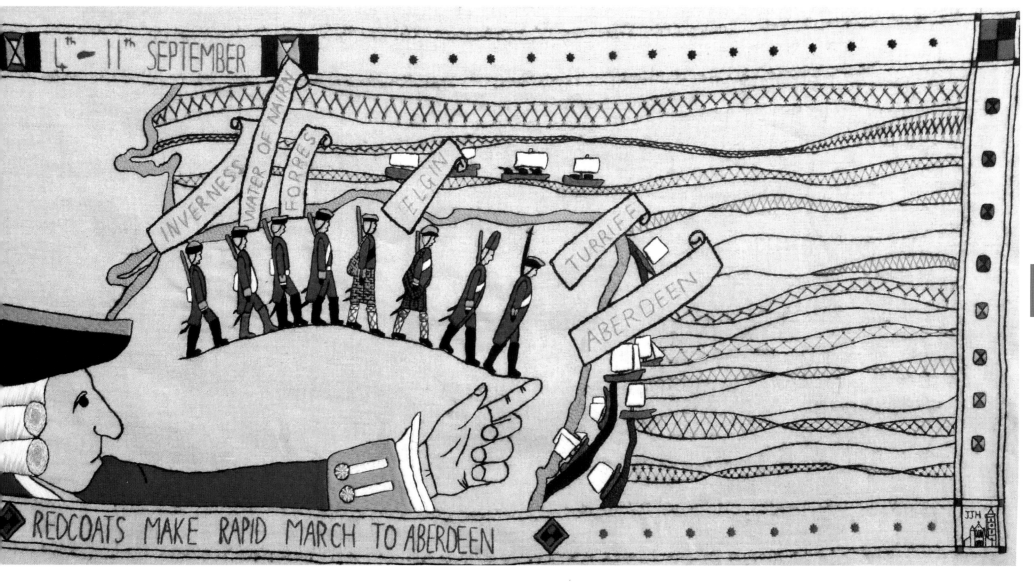

4th – 11th SEPTEMBER

INVERNESS

WATER OF NAIRN

FORRES

ELGIN

TURRIFF

ABERDEEN

REDCOATS MAKE RAPID MARCH TO ABERDEEN

39 The Prince stays at Balhaldie House in Dunblane – September 11th

The Drummond family staying at Balhaldie House was well known to the Jacobites in Paris where a cousin served as a spy on the Stuart's behalf. It was no surprise therefore that, after the Prince left Perth and had briefly visited Scone, when he eventually reached Dunblane on the night of September 11th he lodged, dined and held Council at Balhaldie House. Whilst at Dunblane he was joined by a further 150 clansmen of the Duke of Perth. The town is famed for its 12th century cathedral which at the time was without a roof. Folklore reports that a young maid summoned to the Prince's bed chamber to clean his boots mistakenly assumed it was the boots she should kiss rather than the hand the Prince extended in gratitude.

panel 39

The panel was outline embroidered by Heather Bovill [pictured]. The tag is common to all seven stitched by the team in Dunblane and represents their fine Cathedral. Detailing was embroidered as follows: The Prince Maud Crawford; servant girl Lysbeth Wilson; cathedral tower Mavis Oldham; cathedral pillars/ end windows/ roof Judith Abbott; cathedral windows Mary Storrar; Balhaldie House Jenny Haldane & Mavis Oldham.

THE PRINCE STAYS AT BALHALDIE HOUSE, DUNBLANE

40   Highlanders cross the Forth by the Fords of Frew – September 13th

Leaving Dunblane the Highlanders marched to Doune where the Edmonstone family entertained the Prince at Newton House. On the 13th the Prince was the first to put foot into water and wade out at the head of his detachment as they crossed the Forth at the Fords of Frew. On the appearance of the Highlanders at the Fords Gardiner's dragoons, which had been intended to intercept them, swiftly withdrew to Linlithgow. The Prince paused for refreshments at Leckie House and whilst there sent off a demand to the Provost of Glasgow for £15,000 – which that city steadfastly ignored once they saw the Highlanders were headed towards Stirling.

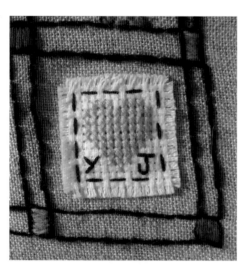

panel 40

This panel was embroidered by Yvonne Johnstone of Port Seton but she stays in The Pans. "I love anything and everything arty and I've studied painting and stitching, embroidery, diy, quilting ... I actually got started on the Battle tapestry jointly with my mother Helen [# 91] but we quickly decided we wanted to create one each. Yet I never ever imagined I'd be stitching so many soldiers!"

13TH SEPTEMBER

CROSSING THE FORDS OF FREW

41 Highlanders by-pass Stirling Castle – September 14th

The Highland army reached Stirling and were entertained by the Provost, but continued their march without injury even though the castle fired upon them. Once again, the Prince had no intention of delaying his progress to Edinburgh ahead of Cope with a seige. Gardiner's failure to oppose the Jacobites at the Fords of Frew had allowed them to clear the only potential major obstacle on their way to the capital with the greatest of ease.

The panel was embroidered [as was #43] by Anne Hamill, Susan Lindsay, Hazel Wood and Gwyneth Hill – the Larbert Group or the 'Desperate Stitchwives' which met every Tuesday. 'The evenings whizzed by with stories of Edinburgh Moon Walking and on the buses! And there were cakes to eat courtesy of McGhee's Bakery and by the time the panel was finished every variety must surely have been savoured. And then there was Hazel's poetry ... for which see #43.

14th SEPTEMBER

HIGHLANDERS BYPASS STIRLING CASTLE

42 The Highlanders capture Falkirk – September 14th

The Highlanders marched directly on towards Falkirk and captured the town with no opposition. En route they had paused briefly, out of respect, at the battlefield of Bannockburn. The Prince then dined at Bannockburn House with Sir Hugh Patterson, uncle to Clementina Walkinshaw, with whom the Prince was subsequently romantically much engaged. [Their liaison was later to create a direct line of descent to Count Peter Pininski in 2010. Four months later Falkirk was to be the scene of the largest battle of the campaign, and the Prince's second victory, this time defeating General Hawley – to Sir John Cope's delight since he had placed a wager with Hawley personally that he too would lose to the Highlanders.]

The panel was embroidered in North Berwick by Halflinbarns Schoolhouse Weaving Group – Vi Bathgate, Jeanette Callaway, Susan Cunningham, Joan Dagg, Frances Fergusson, Frances Gardiner, Elma Learmonth, Beth Orr, Diane Rendalls and Irene Rendalls. The group has been together for 30 years using ancient Egyptian techniques including embroidery. The horse on which the Prince sits was much debated and ultimately agreed as an ancient breed of Irish and Scottish descent using overlay stitches. During our long winter months the light was on all hours and an old saying was a constant reminder to keep going – Ye can either mak a Kirk or a Mill oot o' it. A sense of sharing our history with stitchers across Scotland and appreciating everyone's hidden talents was inspirational.' [Their tag is taken from the remains of the 8th Century High Cross at Aberlady.]

14th SEPTEMBER

THE PRINCE CAPTURES FALKIRK

43   The Prince stays at Callendar House – September 14th

The Prince's host as he stayed overnight at Callendar House was William Boyd, the bankrupt Lord Kilmarnock, who had married into the Livingston family who were tenants there. He offered the Prince his own support and that of his retainers but was unable to persuade any others to come out despite entreaties followed by threats at an assembly in the town hall. This *volte face* followed Kilmarnock's support earlier that very

same day for Gardiner's dragoons whose new positions he at once revealed to Lord George Murray. Murray responded by sending some 500 Highlanders in pursuit for a predawn raid at Linlithgow but found their camp had already been abandoned. The Prince himself accompanied Murray's sortie taking refreshments at Muiravonside.

panel 43

This panel was embroidered as was #41 by Anne Hamill, Susan Lindsay, Hazel Wood and Gwyneth Hill – the Larbert Group, the 'Desperate Stitchwives'. Hazel was moved to poetry [abstracted]... The weather was atrocious, but we couldn't begin/ Until Dorie arrived with material and wool/ We arranged to meet Tuesdays, that was the rule/ So from 7 til 10 we gathered around/ The four of us made not a sound .../ Except to gossip, panic and exclaim/ And to laugh so much we were often in pain/ ... But time is running out and we panic some more/ One panel is finished and our fingers are sore/ ... So here's to the Trust, and celebrations in July/ At Prestonpans, where the flags will fly.

14th SEPTEMBER
LADY ANNE LIVINGSTON
WILLIAM BOYD, EARL OF KILMARNOCK
JACOBITES CAMP BESIDE CALLENDAR HOUSE
SJL AH
GH HW

The Prince stays at Callendar House – September 14th

44   Redcoats prepare the barges in Aberdeen – September 14th

Cope's 'forced' march to Aberdeen had been co-ordinated with the despatch of barges from Leith and the Forth ports to Aberdeen. This meant that on his arrival the redcoats could swiftly embark. The barges did indeed arrive at precisely the time Cope's army reached the town on September 14th. Adverse winds however delayed the departure so he only loaded his supplies immediately. His army stood by ready for embarkation as soon as possible – 'those embarking would include 1600 rank and file, 124 Serjeants and Drummers, 85 Officers, 108 Women and 50 servants, 250 Highlanders, the Train and Horses equal to 400.'

This panel was embroidered by Jacqueline Fawcett who was born in Enfield of paternal Scottish ancestry and is married to David of Scottish maternal ancestry. When they were both made redundant in England in 2006 they moved permanently to their holiday home in France, renovating both house and barn and growing vegetables all year round. Jacqueline has always loved knitting and sewing and even though her first shipped kit was lost in the post was able to complete the work in just ten weeks.

IR JOHN COPE
TRODE THE NORTH RIGHT FAR
YET NE'ER A REBEL
HE CAM NAUR.

REDCOATS BOARD BARGES AT ABERDEEN

45   Sir John Cope sails towards the Forth – September 15th

As soon as the winds changed on the 15th the redcoat army boarded and the barges departed 'on a single tide against all best advice of the Sea People'. Cope fully realised that making good speed could well determine the outcome of the entire campaign. His army got swiftly out of the Bay and headed south to the Forth hoping to reach Leith before the Prince entered Edinburgh but, if that was not possible, to disembark at Dunbar. The earlier hope to disembark at Dundee or Perth had already been frustrated by those ports being dominated by the Prince.

panel
45

This panel was embroidered by Elma Colvin and associates in the final stages of the artwork's preparation. Elma also stitched the Title Panel and # 18. She normally works with silk and dyes designing large wall hangings – often a solitary experience – so 'working with the core team at Cockenzie has been a totally new and exciting experience for me – the scale of it all, the organisation and research involved, working with so many others and learning a great deal more personally about the Battle of Prestonpans. Working together has its own creative magic – and it's fun!'

15th ~ 16th SEPTEMBER   IN ONE TIDE HE EMBARKED THE WHOLE ARMY.   EVEN AGAINST

THE WISHES OF THE SEA PEOPLE

SIR JOHN COPE SAILS TOWARDS THE FORTH

. . . all great works are left unfinished

46 The Highlanders continue their march towards Edinburgh – September 15th

The Highlanders arrived at Linlithgow at 6 am on Sunday 15th but did not occupy the town. The Prince requested that church services be held as usual although the Minister did not do so.

The Prince himself stayed at Linlithgow Palace all day but slept the night three miles east of the town with all his officers and men 'without other covering than their plaids.'

This panel was embroidered by Kathryn Henderson who was born in Inverness and grew up in Culloden. She's been interested in sewing since a young age and came to Edinburgh University in 1999 to study Fine Art/ History of Art with practical classes at the College of Art. Since graduating she has worked and exhibited particularly ink drawings, oil paintings and occasionally textile artworks. As well as practising as an artist she works part-time for the City of Edinburgh Council Museums and Galleries and as a Support Assistant to university students. Her interest in Jacobite Scottish history meant that this tapestry was of immediate interest and she's taken great pleasure in being involved producing her panel.

FALKIRK

15 SEPTEMBER

MARCHING SIX ABREAST

FIRTH OF FORTH

LINLITHGOW

KIRKLISTON

CORSTORPHINE

CRAIGS ROAD

THE HIGHLANDERS MARCH TOWARDS EDINBURGH

47 The Prince sends a Summons to Provost Stewart of Edinburgh demanding the city's surrender – September 16th

The following day the Prince's advance towards Edinburgh continued through Winchburgh and Kirkliston, halting for two hours at Todshall/ Foxhall whilst a reconnoitring party was sent ahead. In the afternoon the Highlanders advanced to Corstorphine, then turning south they encamped at Slateford, the Prince quartering in the home of David Wright, a tacksman, at Gray's Mill on the Waters of Leith. From this camp the Prince sent a summons to the Lord Provost and magistrates of Edinburgh demanding the surrender of the city.

David Wright, the farmer of Gray's Mill, was understandably dismayed to see his crops trampled by the Highlanders and was bold enough to demand compensation which Prince Charles agreed – offering a promissory note payable when the Jacobites were victorious. The canny farmer said he would prefer to have a note from someone he knew. Charles grinned and enquired if he would accept a cheque from the Duke of Perth "who is a more credit-worthy man than I can pretend to be". With distinct relief Wright jumped at the offer.

This panel was embroidered by Caroline Scott and Margaret Burgess. Margaret studied Theatre at the RSAMD in Glasgow and Theatre Design in Bristol and has been engaged in Exhibition Design, and Lecturing in Theatre Arts and Millinery at Edinburgh's Telford College. Caroline Scott studied Fashion Design and Technology at Newcastle upon Tyne Polytechnic and Therapeutic Healing in London. She has taught Fashion at Edinburgh College of Art. Currently, students of Fashion and Business receive further education and opportunity in her company Utterly Bespoke, where she produces Couture Garments for Men and Women using cloths of our Scottish Heritage. Caroline and Margaret have been friends and collegues from when they met through Caroline's company. 'We are both delighted to have sewn this Heritage Tapestry and proud that, through our skills, we contributed to a new Heritage in Scotland'.

16th SEPTEMBER

GRAY'S MILL

COLINTON

HOME OF TACKSMAN DAVID WRIGHT

CORSTORPHINE

CLAYCOTT MAINS FARM

DOVECOT

OLD PARISH CHURCH

DOWER HOUSE

...WE HEREBY SUMMON YOU
TO RECEIVE US AS YOU ARE
DUTY BOUND TO DO.
SUMMON THE TOWN COUNCIL AND TAKE
PROPER MEASURES IN IT FOR
SECURING PEACE AND QUIET OF THE CITY...

THE PRINCE SIGNS A LETTER TO PROVOST STEWART DEMANDING THE SURRENDER OF EDINBURGH

panel 47

The Prince sends a Summons to Provost Stewart of Edinburgh demanding the city's surrender – September 16th

48 Six Volunteer Foot Companies are raised in Edinburgh – September 16th

As the Highlanders approached and the alarm bell had sounded, those who had volunteered to help defend the city congregated in Lawnmarket and they were joined by the Town Guard and the newly formed Edinburgh Regiment. They intended to make their way to Corstorphine to support the dragoons. But the alarm bell had also put an end to church services, and parishioners and ministers alike emerged at once urging family, friends and neighbours who had volunteered *not* to go outside the walls. Eventually Lord Provost Stewart agreed and they were dismissed, except some 180 from the Town Guard and Edinburgh Regiment who did indeed venture out to Corstorphine. But they went out only on the express condition they must return by nightfall.

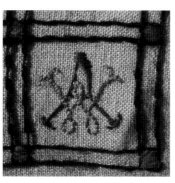

This panel was embroidered by Ageing Well Project of NE Edinburgh – Standing l to r – Ruth Watson/ Robina Brown/ Kath Laing/ Sheila McFarland/ Linda Garcia; Sitting l to r – Mary Stewart/ Laura Kempton-Smith/ Sheila Miller. Edinburgh's Ageing Well Project works in partnership with NHS Lothian, Edinburgh Leisure and Pilmeny Development Project to increase the expectation of good health for those aged over 50. It provides physical activities and social opportunities for older people to enable them to maintain and improve their health through a peer support model. All the projects tackled are led or supported by trained Ageing Well Volunteers. 'We have loved being part of this tapestry – building up the panel into an historic picture and knowing that it will be part of Scotland's history in the years ahead. Our motto "Adding Years to Life and Life to Years" fits in well with Bonnie Prince Charlie's example to commit himself to a cause and to motivate older and wiser men to join him'.

16TH SEPTEMBER

EDINBURGH REGIMENT

ALEXANDER CARLYLE

JOHN HOME

SIX VOLUNTEER FOOT COMPANIES RAISED IN EDINBURGH

49 Redcoat dragoons canter to Colt Bridge then flee east – September 16th

The redcoat dragoons of Gardiner and Hamilton, now commanded by Brigadier General Fowke just arrived from London, had made their way out to Corstophine and as far as Colt Bridge, to reconnoitre the Highland army upon seeing them arrive and camp. However, just as soon as the Prince sent out an advanced party of some 500 towards the dragoons they fled in the greatest haste, and 'in full view of all the populace' on the walls of the city of Edinburgh, making first for Leith and from thence to Musselburgh. This episode was later ridiculed as 'The Canter of Colt Bridge'.

panel 49

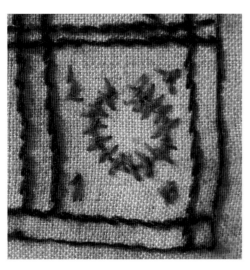

This panel embroidered by Lindsay Young. "My sister Laura introduced me to the tapestry but it was 20 years since I had done a serious piece of work. My grandmother's family lived at Gray's Mill, and she and my mother had inspired me to embroider and knit at an early age. My favourite is the rearing horse but I had fun with the kilts and socks of the 'Blue Bunnets', and deliberately left the faces unfilled to emphasise their expressions. When I read a book describing the actual scene, the whole piece suddenly came alive!"

16 SEPTEMBER

REDCOAT DRAGOONS CANTER AT COLTBRIDGE THEN FLEE TO MUSSELBURGH

Redcoat dragoons canter to Colt Bridge then flee east – September 16th

50 Edinburgh's Lord Provost convenes a Council – September 16th

Seeing the dragoons flee east of the city the alarm bell was again sounded and the populace of Edinburgh was summoned to Goldsmith's Hall. Such was the crowd it was moved to the New Church in St Giles Cathedral. Lord Provost Stewart had by now received the Prince's summons to surrender the city, and reluctantly read it out aloud. Rumour-mongers had it that there were as many as 16,000 Highlanders at the gates, which was a ridiculous exaggeration. Realising that resistance was likely to be in vain, the citizens resolved to send a deputation to the Prince to discuss the surrender terms. It left for Gray's Mill at around 8 pm.

panel 50

This panel was embroidered by a team from Edinburgh's Ageing Well Project which works in partnership with NHS Lothian, Edinburgh Leisure and Pilmeny Development Project to increase the expectation of good health for those aged over 50. It provides physical activities and social opportunities for older people to enable them to maintain and improve their health through a peer support model. All the projects tackled are led or supported by trained Ageing Well Volunteers. 'We have loved being part of this tapestry – building up the panel into an historic picture and knowing that it will be part of Scotland's history in the years ahead. Our motto "Adding Years to Life and Life to Years" fits in well with Bonnie Prince Charlie's example to commit himself to a cause and to motivate older and wiser men to join him'. The team appears: Back l to r. - Robina Brown/ Ruth Watson/ Kath Laing; Seated l to r - Mary Stewart/ Laura Kempton-Smith/ Sheila Miller/ Sheila McFarland/ Linda Garcia.

15th SEPTEMBER

PROVOST STEWART

EDINBURGHS LORD PROVOST AND COUNCIL MEET

51 Edinburgh's Lord Provost seeks to negotiate with the Prince but receives an ultimatum – September 16th

The Provost's deputation were refused admission to the Prince. Through his Secretary Murray of Broughton the Prince affirmed orally and in writing that he would not negotiate with his father's subjects. However, the Prince agreed to give them two to three hours to consult with their constituents on whether to surrender or fight. Before the deputation had returned, however, Cope's barges had been sighted from Edinburgh arriving at Dunbar giving those in the capital some hope that a 'treasonable' surrender of the city might be avoided. An effort was even made to try to recall the deputation to the Prince. But the recall came too late and the deputies arrived back in Edinburgh at 10 pm with the Prince's uncompromising message of 'no negotiation'. To seek further delay the Lord Provost now contrived to send a second deputation.

panel 51

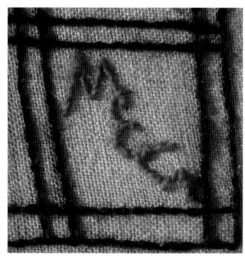

This panel was embroidered by Maeve Greer, who has been interested in all forms of embroidery from a young age. Born in Ireland, she came to Edinburgh to study for a Degree in Commerce. Since Graduating she divides her time between working in administration and gardening and finds sewing relaxing. She has stitched many different types of handwork including tapestry, blackwork, cross stitch and embroidery. Also stitched #52. "The whole project has given a fresh insight in the history of the times" and it has been thoroughly enjoyable.

Text within the tapestry image:

16th SEPTEMBER — GOLDSMITH HALL — GENERAL GUEST — JUSTICE CLERK LORD MILTON — LORD ADVOCATE ROBERT CRAIGIE — SOLICITOR GENERAL ROBERT DUNDAS — DEPUTATION — PROVOST STEWART SEEKS TO NEGOTIATE BUT RECEIVES ULTIMATUM

Edinburgh's Lord Provost seeks to negotiate with the Prince but receives an ultimatum – September 16th

52 Highlanders enter Edinburgh at night by Netherbow Gate – September 17th

The Prince was also aware of Cope's arrival off Dunbar and took immediate steps to capture Edinburgh. As soon as the first deputation had left he sent Lochiel, O'Sullivan and Keppoch with some 800/ 900 picked men [with Murray of Broughton as guide] to seize the city by stealth. When the Provost's second deputation eventually reached the Prince at 2 am he turned them immediately away and it was their return to Edinburgh that gave Lochiel his opportunity. When the deputation's coach was on its way back to its stables at 5 am, via the Netherbow Gate, the concealed Highlanders swarmed through that gate as it opened and were in the city. Whilst its inhabitants slept Edinburgh accordingly fell to the Prince without any bloodshed. Only the castle with General Guest commanding remained in redcoat hands.

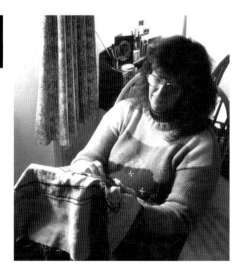

This panel was embroidered by Maeve Greer, who has been interested in all forms of embroidery from a young age. Born in Ireland, she came to Edinburgh to study for a Degree in Commerce. Since Graduating she divides her time between working in administration and gardening and finds sewing relaxing. She has stitched many different types of handwork including tapestry, blackwork, cross stitch and embroidery. Also stitched #51. "The whole project has given a fresh insight in the history of the times" and it has been thoroughly enjoyable.

17th SEPTEMBER

HIGHLANDERS ENTER EDINBURGH AT NIGHT BY NETHERBOW GATE

Highlanders enter Edinburgh at night by Netherbow Gate – September 17th

53 The Prince enters the Palace of Holyroodhouse – September 17th

Just five hours after the Highlanders entered Edinburgh at the Netherbow Gate, the Prince himself arrived at 10 am. He came by the southeast to avoid the lowering guns of the castle which nonetheless fired a few desultory rounds. Then the Highlanders marched north to arrive in King's Park at the walls of Holyrood. A vast crowd welcomed him. From amongst the crowd, one James Hepburn of Keith took it upon himself to precede the Prince with raised sword as he approached the Palace entrance – the first royal person so to do since his grandfather, the future King James II and VII, had stayed there more than 60 years before as Viceroy of Scotland. The Prince occupied hastily prepared rooms.

This panel was embroidered by Shona McManus, born on the Isle of Harris and brought up with the romantic image of Bonnie Prince Charlie including many great Jacobite songs. 'The true purpose of the Prince's campaign in 1745 was not well told to us but my husband was intrigued by the Prestonpans tapestry initiative and persuaded me to volunteer.' The embroidery has been a most rewarding cultural and educational experience with the opportunity to join an inspiring, talented and dedicated team. My tag remembers my brave and loyal little dog JED – which stands for Jacobite Endurance and Dedication. He was as brave as The Prince himself.'

17TH SEPTEMBER

JAMES HEPBURN or KEITH

PRINCE ENTERS HOLYROOD PALACE

54   Sir John Cope lands at Dunbar – September 17th

Cope learnt of Edinburgh's capture whilst still aboard ship off Dunbar. He was met as he landed by the dragoons whose flight was now complete. They were in total disarray. It took Cope two days to disembark which fortunately afforded time for the dragoons to rest. Cope was in two minds as to how soon he should march on Edinburgh, particularly aware that Dutch and British reinforcements were on their way. So he called a Council and Colonel Gardiner amongst others argued strongly that they should await such reinforcements. But Cope felt delay would give succour to the Highlanders whose numbers would grow further. He wished to reach Edinburgh as swiftly as possible and had a pre-agreed plan with General Guest and the redcoats in the castle as to how an attack could be successfully made.

panel 54

This panel was embroidered by Ena Cunningham of Dunbar. She learnt of the tapestry when she got chatting at the Trust's 2009 Battle Ceilidh and, since she had some sewing experience, volunteered at once. Her daughter-in-law was also embroidering a panel so together they got to know a great deal of 'new' history about the Prince's campaign. Ena's husband Bob was detailed to locate 'Cope's Steps' where his redcoats came ashore in 1745 at Dunbar Harbour and what he found is on the panel.

17th SEPTEMBER — COPE SENT A CHALLENGE FRAE DUNBAR

SIR JOHN COPE LANDS AT DUNBAR — CHARLIE MEET ME AN' YE DAUR

JOHNNY COPE STEPS

CROMWELL HARBOUR

CRC

55 King James VIII and III Proclaimed at Edinburgh's Mercat Cross – September 17th

At 12 noon the Prince accompanied by Lyon Court Heralds and the Heralds and the magistrates made his way to Edinburgh's Mercat Cross where the Highlanders formed a circle six deep. King James VIII and III and the Commission of Regency for the Prince were both proclaimed by Ross Herald, together with the Prince's Manifesto, to a great crowd of thousands. The populace of Edinburgh was hanging from the windows, *'it all amidst much cheering, huzzaing and waving of ladies' handkerchiefs'*. One of those watching was Magdalen [Maddie] Pringle, a young lass visiting the city. Although her family were not Jacobites, she was swept away by the excitement, 'stalking' the Prince's every move. It was she who first refers to the Prince as *'bonny'* and in her letters spelt out what fashions she felt suited him best. She wrote to her sister Isabella [Tibbie] on September 18th : *"Ye windows were full of Ladys who threw up their handkerchiefs and clap'd their hands, show'd great loyalty to ye Bonny Prince"*.

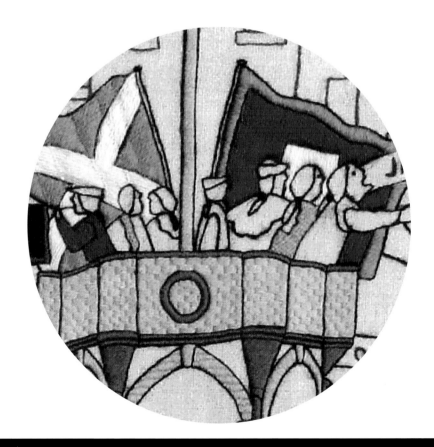

This panel was embroidered by Celia Mainland who recently moved to Prestonpans after a career in public administration in Shetland, Edinburgh, London and Belfast. Born in Newcastle, she graduated from Edinburgh which she now regards as her 'home' city. She enjoys music, the arts, genealogy, gardening and cooking. One of her most treasured possessions is an 1866 tapestry sampler made by her great-grandmother.

56 Highland Army camps in The King's Park – September 17th

The King's Park provided ample space for the ever growing numbers of the Highlanders and it was out of range of the castle's cannons under General Guest's command. They were joined by 400 MacLachlans and men from Atholl under Lord Nairne's command. The city of Edinburgh also provided 1200 muskets for the Highland army on the Prince's demand once news of Cope's landing at Dunbar was received. Lord Provost Stewart was further required to provide 1000 tents, 6000 pairs of shoes and 6000 canteens. The army subsequently moved its camp to Duddingston on September 19th.

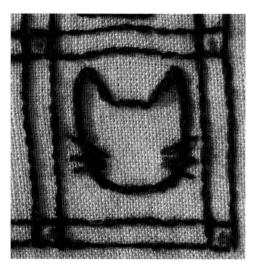

This panel was embroidered by Elizabeth Couper who stitched it in sight of Arthur's Seat from her home. 'I will now see it and the Crags quite differently having closely studied the shades used by nature in the vegetation and the rocks. It was my first attempt at crewel work and I hope in future to solve one of life's great mysteries – why does the length of wool always run out with just a few stitches to go? Thanks to my 17 year old cat and very supportive husband who both behaved impeccably whilst I was concentrating on my panel'.

17th SEPTEMBER

HIGHLANDER ARMY CAMP IN KINGS PARK

57 The Prince holds a Council of War in Duddingston – September 19th

The Highlanders were eager to do battle with Cope. The Prince and Clan Chiefs met in War Council at The Cottage in Duddingston and took refreshments at the Sheep Heid. The Council had three issues to discuss – [i] should they await Cope in Edinburgh; [ii] how the clans should form in battle line respecting ancient rights and privileges; and [iii] whether the men would relish the fight when the time came and if so whether the Prince could lead them into battle. They resolved to go out and do battle immediately, but all were clear that the Prince must be held safely at all times.

This panel was embroidered by Meg Porteous of Edinburgh. Meg has had a lifelong love of knitting and sewing and has produced many lovely tapestries and cross stitched pictures. Her most challenging work was a large copy of the 15C French tapestry "The Vintage" and she has also made very fine reproductions of Georgian carpets for her dolls house. "I have found this project fascinating and have met some super people; I have a love of Scotland and I'm proud to be part of this historic work." Her late husband was also a proud Scot and he would have shown a keen interest in this tapestry. Meg's tag is of a rhododendron as growing them was one of his many hobbies.

19th SEPTEMBER

COLONEL ALEXANDER MACDONALD KEPPOCH

DUKE OF PERTH

SIR JOHN MACDONALD

LORD GEORGE MURRAY

JW SULLIVAN

LORD DAVID WEMYSS ELCHO

COLONEL DONALD CAMERON OF LOCHIEL

SHEEP HEID

THE PRINCE HOLDS COUNCIL OF WAR AT THE CAUSEWAY IN DUDDINGSTON

The Prince holds a Council of War in Duddingston – September 19th

58 Redcoat army marches from Dunbar to Haddington – September 19th

His troops rested, Cope resolved to march towards Edinburgh and on September 19th covered the 11 miles to Haddington, arriving at midday and resolving to stay the night since water was not readily available further west. That evening Cope met George Drummond, a former Lord Provost of Edinburgh, and several of the Edinburgh Volunteers who had made their way to Linton the previous day. He declined the latter's military services but invited them to scout for him at which they were spectacularly unsuccessful. Two of them unwisely fell into the hands of John Roy Stewart's Highlanders whilst breakfasting on wine and Pandores oysters but were soon released. Cope gave orders to be ready to depart from Haddington at 9 am on September 20th.

This panel was embroidered by Frances Gardiner of North Berwick. Frances originally misheard artist Andrew Crummy saying the redcoats were marching along the old Post Road, thinking it was the Coast Road which passed her home. No matter. As they marched the soldiers must have observed many ruined castles and prominent landmarks along their route. The array of lovely wool colours soon became tapsalteerie in hand at home, and the route map began to have a life of its own. Confidence rose as we became historically more informed. During long winter months the light was on at all hours. The sense of sharing in a celebration of our history with "stitchers" throughout Scotland and beyond and appreciating everyone's hidden talents was inspirational. It has been a truly happy time.

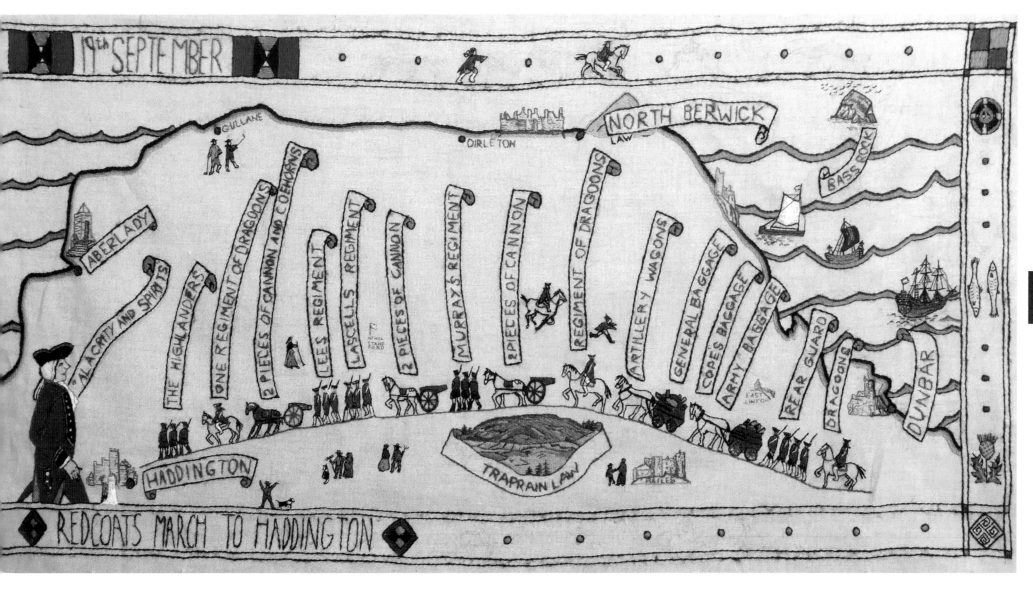

19th SEPTEMBER

GULLANE

DIRLETON

NORTH BERWICK LAW

BASS ROCK

ABERLADY

ALACRITY AND SPIRITS

THE HIGHLANDERS

ONE REGIMENT OF DRAGOONS

2 PIECES OF CANNON AND COEHORNS

LEES REGIMENT

LASCELLS REGIMENT

2 PIECES OF CANNON

MURRAYS REGIMENT

2 PIECES OF CANNON

REGIMENT OF DRAGOONS

ARTILLERY WAGONS

GENERAL BAGGAGE

COPES BAGGAGE

ARMY BAGGAGE

REAR GUARD

DRAGOONS

DUNBAR

ATHEL STANE FORD

EAST LINTON

HADDINGTON

TRAPRAIN LAW

HAILES

REDCOATS MARCH TO HADDINGTON

Redcoat army marches from Dunbar to Haddington – September 19th

59   The Prince meets Beatrix Jenkinson and her sister Mary at The Cottage – September 19th

The Jenkinson sisters, Beatrix and Mary, were staying at Tranent Manse with their brother and their father – who was Minister at Athelstaneford. Hearing of the excitement the Highlanders had created and particularly wishing to see the Prince, the two sisters had travelled to Duddingston where the Prince noticed them. So entranced was he by them that he gave them each a gift, a snuff box and a diamond ring from his own finger, declaring them to be *"the bonniest lassies I have yet seen in Scotland"*.

This panel was embroidered by Ruth McAlpine from Eskbank, Midlothian, where she has lived for 26 years with her husband Kenny. Following her retirement after a 33 year career with The City of Edinburgh Council, she was encouraged to embroider a panel by her neighbour Dorie Wilkie. Having only ever previously worked in cross stitch, making samplers for friends and colleagues, completing this panel was a very considerable challenge. However, being involved in such a project which will have huge historical significance, has proved to be an extremely inspiring experience.

THE PRINCE MEETS BEATRIX JENKINSON AND HER SISTER AT THE COTTAGE

SHEEP HEID INN

The Prince meets Beatrix Jenkinson and her sister Mary at The Cottage – September 19th

60 Redcoats march to Prestonpans and marshal their foot soldiers, cannons and dragoons ready for battle – September 20th

As Cope marched from Haddington towards Edinburgh he understood the Highlanders were encamped at Duddingston. He expected them to remain there and resolved to reach Musselburgh so he could storm the city. General Guest's garrison would then break out from the castle as pre-planned. He followed the post road as far as Elvingston where he veered off north west to the coast and low lying fields where his dragoons and artillery could be effective. As he approached Musselburgh he sent out a scouting party including the Earls of Loudon and Home and Lord Drummore. To their surprise they saw, through their field glasses, firstly Strathallan's cavalry, then closely following the entire Jacobite army on the march. Cope immediately resolved to form up on the open ground between Prestonpans, Seton and Tranent to face them. He had Preston House and Bankton House in front with the Forth to his right flank and marshy ground to his left. The land was bisected by a coal waggonway and a cart track, both running between Tranent and Cockenzie.

panel 60

This panel was embroidered by Margaret Studley with support from Carmel Daly. Margaret's interest in embroidery was fostered by her mother and maintained, as a hobby, throughout her career as a nurse. Retirement has allowed her to further develop her skills and she is currently working towards the City and Guilds in Creative Design – of embroidery.

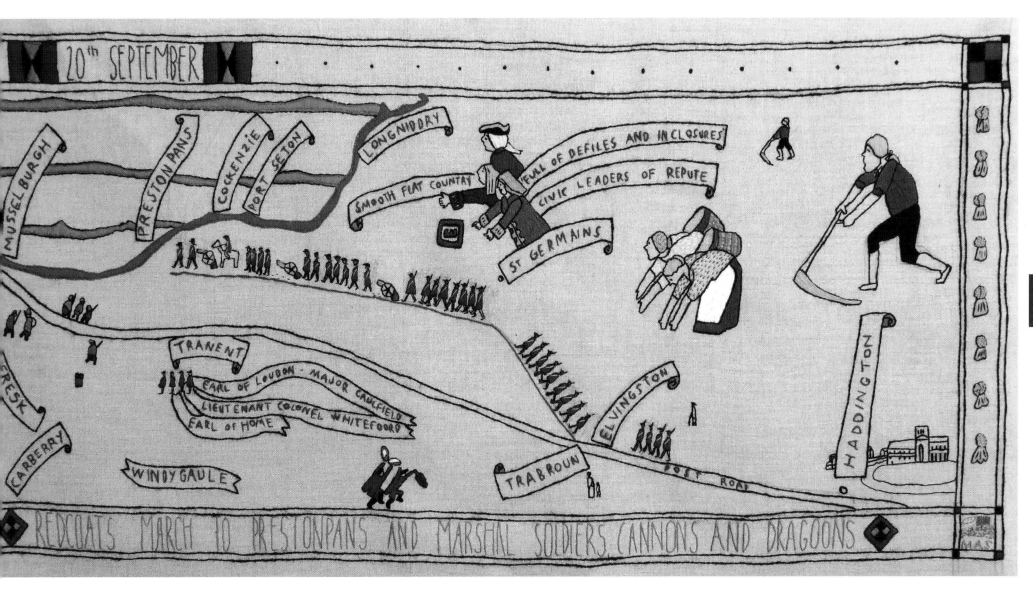

20th SEPTEMBER

MUSSELBURGH
PRESTONPANS
COCKENZIE
PORT SETON
LONGNIDDRY
SMOOTH FLAT COUNTRY
FULL OF DEFILES AND INCLOSURES
CIVIC LEADERS OF REPUTE
ST GERMAINS
FRESK
TRANENT
EARL OF LOUDON - MAJOR CAULFIELD
LIEUTENANT COLONEL WHITEFOORD
EARL OF HOME
CARBERRY
WINDYGAULE
TRABROUN
ELVINGSTON
POST ROAD
HADDINGTON

panel 60

REDCOATS MARCH TO PRESTONPANS AND MARSHAL SOLDIERS, CANNONS AND DRAGOONS

Redcoats march to Prestonpans and marshal their foot soldiers, cannons and dragoons ready for battle – September 20th

61 The Highland army marches to Musselburgh and crosses the Roman Bridge – September 20th

The Highland army had left Duddingston early in the morning on September 20th with the Prince drawing his sword dramatically and declaring: *"Gentleman, I have flung away the scabbard. Cope shall not escape us as he did in the Highlands."* The Strathallan Horse led the army followed by the Camerons. They crossed the Esk at Musselburgh via the Roman Bridge and passed Pinkie House, the home of Lord Tweeddale, the Secretary of State for North Britain. Then Strathallan's scouts spotted the redcoats near Tranent and two prisoners scouting for Cope from the Edinburgh Volunteers were brought in by Colonel Roy Stewart.

panel 61

This panel was embroidered by members of Craft Clinic, who meet every Thursday at the Fisherrow Centre. 'We all have a passion for crafting and find activities such as beading, felting and knitting very therapeutic and a good way to let off steam, so when we saw the advert calling for stitchers we thought we'd give it a go. Naturally, we were drawn to the two panels which depict iconic landmarks in our home town of Musselburgh: the Roman Bridge, shown here, and Pinkie House which appears later in the book. We worked on the panel in shifts, often burning the midnight oil and neglecting our families in the process! Many of us had never embroidered before but as time wore on we became hooked on the craft, learning new stitches and becoming more confident. The end result represents a huge effort on behalf of the group and we are very proud. Stitchers include Gaynor and Imogen Allen, Karen Fiddler, Sue Henderson, Karyn Malcolm-Smith and Laura Young.'

20TH SEPTEMBER · GENTLEMEN, I HAVE FLUNG AWAY THE SCABBARD

POST ROAD · DUDDINGSTON · MAGDALENE BRIDGE · ROMAN BRIDGE · PINKIE HOUSE · BUANT EDGE BRAE · INVERESK · FA'SIDE CASTLE · BIRSLIE BRAE

HIGHLAND ARMY MARCHES TO BIRSLIE BRAE AND TRANENT

panel
61

62 The Highlanders pass through Inveresk en route to Birslie Brae – September 20th

The intelligence received suggested [wrongly] that Cope was headed for the high ground at Falside Hill. Lord George Murray was determined to prevent this. On his own initiative he gathered the Camerons and headed past Inveresk across the fields to Carberry Hill where he paused at 2pm for the others to catch up. They proceeded west together as far as Birslie Brae leaving the Strathallan Horse behind on the Prince's command to block Cope's way to Edinburgh. As the Highlanders looked down to the north, somewhat to their surprise, they saw Cope's army just 800 yards away but 150 feet below on level ground.

This panel was created by Marianne More-Gordon assisted by fellow members of the Inveresk Sewing Group. The group has worked together since Queen Elizabeth's Jubilee when they made a quilt that is today in the Palace of Holyroodhouse. They normally make pieces for charities and the Battle Trust's tapestry had especial fascination since several of the members of the group live in houses depicted in the tapestry. They couldn't resist the challenge.

20TH SEPTEMBER

ALEXANDER CARLYLE

panel
62

THE HIGHLANDERS PASS THROUGH INVERESK EN ROUTE TO BIRSLEY BRAE

63 Redcoats wheel south to face the Highlanders across the marshlands – September 20th

The arrival of the Highlanders on the high ground towards Tranent did not greatly concern Cope since the ditches and marshland at the foot of Birslie Brae and Tranent made any charge down hill impractical. Nonetheless he wheeled his army from its position facing west to face south and advanced it 100 yards to the ditches thus directly facing the Highlanders. They were now in full view of one another across marshland and meadow, with the Highlanders 150 feet above on the ridge.

Each side hurled defiant cheers at the other. Colonel Ker was sent by Lord George Murray to reconnoitre the meadows and was shot at by Cope's men beyond the ditch. Ker returned to confirm what Murray already suspected – that it was impossible to pass the ditches in line. The high ground could not give the Highlanders the advantage originally anticipated when Murray had diverted across the fields from Musselburgh earlier in the day.

This panel was embroidered by Margaret Ewan and Margaret Caldwell of Burntisland in Fife who volunteered via the Scottish Costume Society. They both have a deep interest in arts and crafts – jewellery, silversmithing, historic costumes and knitting but only a little skill at embroidery at the outset. Margaret Ewan is a dedicated Highlander but they fell for their redcoat drummer. The tag is Margaret Ewan's own dog.

20TH SEPTEMBER "WHILE GENERAL COPE DID TAUNT AND MOCK,

WI MONY A LOUD HUZZA, MAN." SKIRVING

◆ REDCOATS WHEEL SOUTH TO FACE THE HIGHLANDERS ACROSS THE MARSHLANDS ◆

Redcoats wheel south to face the Highlanders across the marshlands – September 20th

64 Camerons occupy Tranent churchyard and exchange fire with redcoat cannon – September 20th

Whilst Colonel Ker was testing the redcoats' defensive ditches, O'Sullivan took the initiative to send a party of Camerons further west through Tranent to occupy the churchyard. It was a strong defensible position and a sensible outpost to occupy. However, the Camerons were approached by an independent solo scouting mission, one Customs Collector Walter Grossett, and they unwisely fired on him thus giving away their position. Grossett reported back to Cope who sent cannon forward to lay fire on the churchyard wounding several of the Camerons.

This panel was embroidered by Judith Abbott. A student in Edinburgh she came to stay in Dunblane where she's now been for forty years – learning & developing needlework skills in local groups and for the National Trust's work at Falkland Palace. She was a member of a volunteer group stitching several panels in Dunblane.

20th SEPTEMBER

CAMERONS OCCUPY TRANENT CHURCH AND EXCHANGE FIRE WITH REDCOAT CANNON

panel 64

65 Lochiel withdraws his Camerons from the churchyard – September 20th

Neither Lochiel or Murray had been aware of O'Sullivan's decision to send the Camerons forward to the churchyard. Both were greatly annoyed. Lochiel, without consulting O'Sullivan, insisted his men were withdrawn before any further casualties occurred. This in turn angered O'Sullivan who argued the Highlanders were leaving their flank exposed. Nonetheless the movement farther east that the Camerons had started was now followed at nightfall by all the Highlanders with the exception of the Strathallan Horse which was already posted between Edinburgh and Cope's army west of Bankton House. The Horse remained a while longer before moving across to Dolphinstoun. The redcoats could not see the movements of the main body of Highlanders to the east but loudly barking dogs in Tranent at around 9 pm were readily interpreted to have been caused by significant troop movements.

This panel was embroidered by Mavis Oldham of Dunblane. Mavis was sewing before she started school and has always been active since including several projects with the Scottish WI Rurals. A City & Guilds graduate in embroidery and design she has taught for 35 years and been a member of the Embroiderers Guild for 34, pleased to play her part in keeping the craft alive.

20th SEPTEMBER

LOCHIEL WITHDRAWS CAMERONS FROM CHURCHYARD

66 Robert Anderson demonstrates a route through the marshland – September 20th

The Highlanders in Council concluded that the only line of attack they could now make would involve moving much farther east and descending to the fields below. But the question was just how far east they needed to go before they could circumvent the marshy land. If they were unable to arrive until late in the morning Cope would have ample time to prepare or he could drive on to Edinburgh. One of the Prince's young local officers, Robert Anderson of Whitburgh, knew of an excellent solution. His father owned the meadowlands and there was a little known route which he used when hunting. Anderson was too diffident to make the case until urged, after the Council disbanded, by his friend James Hepburn of Keith – this was the man who had spontaneously preceded the Prince into Holyrood just three days before [Panel #53].

panel
66

This panel was embroidered by Greta Anderson, a Panner born and bred. She stitched this panel in memory of her late husband Robert, namesake of the young man who guided the Prince past Riggonhead Farm to Victory on September 21st 1745. Her treble clef tag represents her husband's 40 years in the Brass Band movement. Greta has thoroughly enjoyed the work, meeting stitchers from all over Scotland in the process – making an intriguing change from her regular hobby of card making with friends and a good blether.

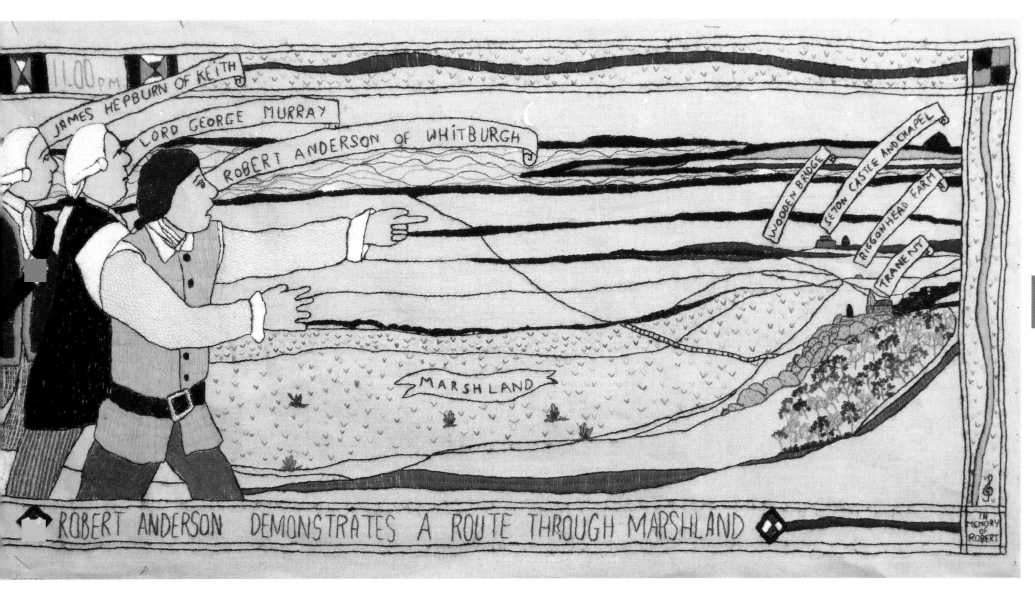

panel 66

Robert Anderson demonstrates a route through the marshland – September 20th

67   The Prince in Council agrees to move along the Riggonhead Defile – September 20th

Robert Anderson woke Lord George Murray to give him the information on the little known route through the marshlands. Murray was immediately impressed and roused the Prince who was asleep close by on a 'sheaf of peas'. The Council was reconvened at midnight and swiftly resolved to follow the route Anderson had pinpointed. As had been agreed earlier at Duddingston [Panel # 57], the MacDonalds were to take the lead, which necessitated passing by the Camerons who were already farthest east. In this way the MacDonalds were positioned to become the coveted Highland right flank when the battle line was drawn on the fields below. This was accomplished with the 'least noise and confusion' by 4 am. The route they were to follow went past Riggonhead Farm then along what became known as the Riggonhead Defile, the Highlanders emerging to the west of Seton Collegiate church.

This panel's embroidery was co-ordinated by Lyn Dunachie working with friends in the Strathendrick Branch of the Embroiderers Guild. They come from central Scotland – Helensburgh and Balloch, Bishopbriggs and Kikintilloch, Glasgow, Paisley and Stirling – to meet in Killearn. In the photograph they are, [l/r], Phyllis Hardie, Lyn Dunachie, Pam Waller, Christina McLachlan (seated), Margaret Burgess, Marlene Coleman (in front), Susan Rhind, Margaret Harrison, Christine Gastall, Sandy LePla and not pictured Margaret Sutherland.

MIDNIGHT

THE PRINCE WAS SLEEPING ON A SHEAF OF PEAS

PRINCE IN COUNCIL AGREES TO MOVE ALONG RIGGONHEAD DEFILE

The Prince in Council agrees to move along the Riggonhead Defile – September 20th

68　The redcoats set pickets overnight – September 20th/21st

Cope had readily identified that the only sensible direction of attack for the Highlanders was from the east. At night he accordingly posted some 500 men, 200 dragoons and 300 foot soldiers, as outguard pickets to the east, and on the waggonway and farm track running south/north through the marshy lands. Pickets also went to the ditches and to the base of Fa'side Hill. But all remained totally unaware of Robert

Anderson's route past Riggonhead Farm towards Seton. The pickets reported to Cope half hourly throughout the night. Three fires were lit at the front of the redcoat lines so that the outguards could see more clearly. One mortar was fired off at the Highlanders' lines in Tranent when troop movements were detected although it failed to explode through damnification.

panel 68

This panel was embroidered by Norah Anderson and Theena Anderson. Norah and Theena have been needlewomen all their lives although whilst Theena learnt as a wee girl and took City & Guilds at Esk Valley College Norah came to stitching when falling ill with TB as a teenager. Both do patchwork and enjoy embroidery as embellishment and found working together on this panel challenging but most rewarding.

GROUND AND BEYOND

...00 DRAGOONS AND 300 FOOT ~ WERE DEPLOYED AS OUTGUARDS AND REPORTED TO COPE EVERY HALF HOUR

...SING OVER THE ENTIRE GROUND AND BEYOND TO THE

BASE OF FALSIDE HILL ON THE FARSIDE OF THE MARSH NEAR TO THE REBELS

AND TO THE EAST ~ BRINGING GOOD INTELLIGENCE THE WHOLE

NIGHT, OF EVERY MOTION

THE ENEMY MADE

COPE SETS PICKETS OVERNIGHT

N.A.
T.D.A

69 Highlanders march three abreast along the Riggonhead Defile – September 21st

Once the MacDonalds had reached their position at the head of the Highland army, the army could all move off. It was just after 4 am and Robert Anderson was out front – just starlight and the moon allowing them to see their way. In the first column, under the command of the Duke of Perth, marched the Clanranalds then the Glengarrys, some Grants and finally the Keppochs and MacDonalds of Glencoe. The second column, under command of Lord George Murray, consisted of Perth's own regiment, the MacGregors, with the Appin Stewarts and Lochiel's Camerons. The rear column, the Reserve, included the Menzies, the Atholl Brigade quietly behind, the MacLachlans under Lord Nairne, the Robertson's and the Prince in person.

It was a mile north along the defile to Riggonhead Farm where they turned northwest, shortly thereafter crossing a four foot ditch. The Prince deliberately ignored the bridge to leap the ditch but stumbled and was immediately helped across.

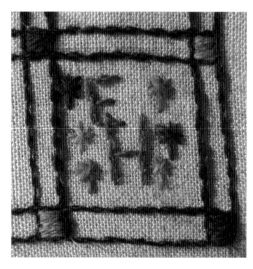

panel 69

This panel was embroidered by Elaine McMorrine, lifelong friend of the Lead Stitcher – so a natural recruit. "All my life I have worked as a nurse and looked after our children. I've always loved sewing but had not done any for years – what a great challenge, I thought. How right. After buying a book on stitches I became more confident and found it a relaxing challenge, de-stressing even. I feel proud I can tell our grandchildren this will be part of Scottish history – especially as they live in England!

'THE ENTIRE FORCE, MINUS STRATHALLAN'S CAVALRY, BEGAN ITS EASTWARD MARCH'

4.00 AM

HIGHLANDERS MARCH THREE ABREAST THROUGH THE NIGHT AS SUN RISES

70 Redcoat pickets challenge the Highlanders in the morning mist and flee – September 21st

The Duke of Perth's first column passed undetected through the Riggonhead Defile and turning northwest crossed the fields of Seton Mains arriving some 500/ 600 yards to the east of where the waggonway and cart track intersected. The second column commanded by Lord George Murray encountered a picket of dragoons as it emerged from the marshes but did not respond when challenged, and it too proceeded onto the field, with the the Prince in the Reserve behind. The dragoons on the picket lines fled back to Cope with their alarming news.

This panel was embroidered by Vennetta Evans whose grandfather, a Campbell, came from Peebles, although Vennetta moved as recently as 2008 to East Lothian from Gloucestershire. Her 'nightime' panel led her to careful research to identify where the moon and stars were in the sky that September night in 1745 with the answer finally coming from the French Astronomical Society! The project has been characterised by bags of enthusiasm and the opportunity to learn a great deal more about Scotland's history.

WHICH KING ? WHICH KING ?

ALARM ALARM ALARM ALARM ALARM

DRAGOON PICKETS CHALLENGE THE HIGHLANDERS THEN FLEE

71 Alerted, Sir John Cope wheels his army to face east – September 21st

As soon as the dragoons reported the Highlanders' presence to the east Cope ordered his signal gun to be fired. This at once ensured the withdrawal of all his outguards and pickets and the arousal of the remainder of his army. Cope then wheeled his entire force from its positions facing south to face east, with his artillery of six cannons, four coehorns and two royals all on his right flank. After this was completed, the redcoat line extended just short of 700 paces from end to end – a magnificent and fearsome sight to any enemy.

panel 71

This panel was embroidered by Linda Jobson of Eskbank, a lover of thread and colour. She kept a diary as the stitching went along [looks daunting; first stitch made with trepidation; one of Sir John's boots took 2 hours], concluding with the entry: 'I'm elated with my achievement and proud to have been involved. It's been a labour of love and my tag symbolises my love of nature!'

ALERTED SIR JOHN COPE WHEELS HIS ARMY TO FACE EAST

72   Map of the Battle Lines – September 21st 1745

The positions of the Clans and Regiments are shown. The dragoons actually stood behind the redcoat foot soldiers, which had all the artillery on their right flank. The Highlanders on their own right flank under the Duke of Perth had actually travelled much farther than anticipated and outflanked the redcoats. The Reserve in the centre, including the Prince, was accordingly in direct line of vision to the redcoats as the Highlanders' charge took place although it was still consider-ably behind the front line and at no time entered combat.

[Battlefield archaeology in 2009/ 2010 by the Trust strongly suggests that the first engagements on the Highlanders' right flank took place to the east of the waggonway and cart track in the area known as Seton Farm East. On their left flank the Camerons engagement with Cope's artillery was somewhat closer to the waggonway itself.]

This panel was embroidered by Elizabeth Jones of Prestonpans where she has lived all her life. She became involved as an embroiderer with the Battle Trust following the 2009 re-enactments in Cuthill Park and her panel was the very first to be completed – in January 2010. Elizabeth has been a key member of the Cockenzie team throughout and dedicates her panel to her 'wonderful' husband Stuart and their five children Mark, Christopher, Emma, Liam and Shaun

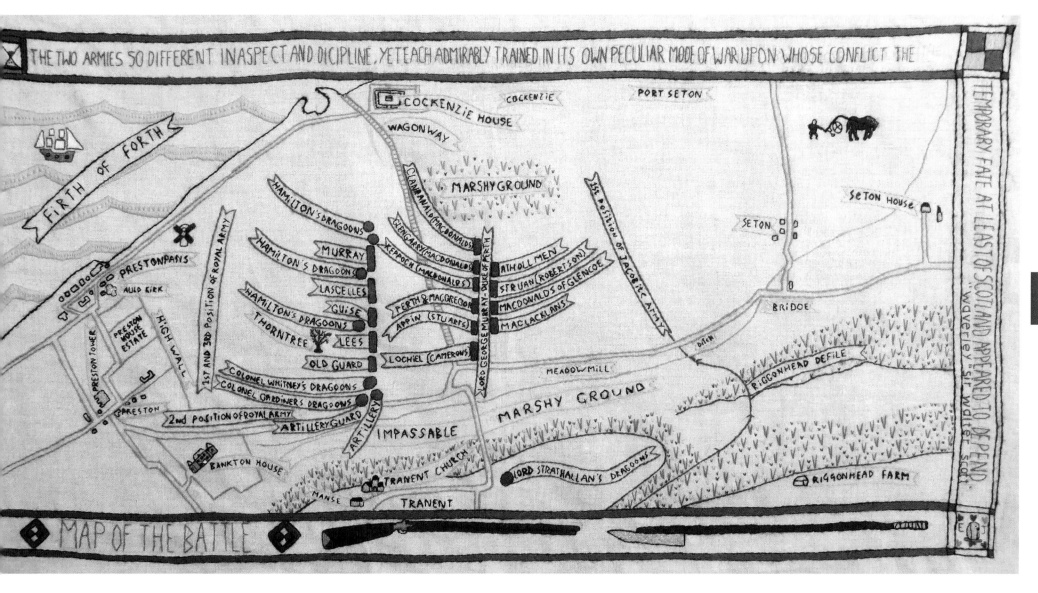

THE TWO ARMIES SO DIFFERENT IN ASPECT AND DICIPLINE, YET EACH ADMIRABLY TRAINED IN ITS OWN PECULIAR MODE OF WAR UPON WHOSE CONFLICT THE

FIRTH OF FORTH

COCKENZIE HOUSE
COCKENZIE
PORT SETON
WAGON WAY

MARSHY GROUND

CLANRANALD (MACDONALDS)

PRESTONPANS
AULD KIRK

HAMILTON'S DRAGOONS
MURRAY
HAMILTON'S DRAGOONS
LASCELLES
HAMILTON'S DRAGOONS
GUISE
THORNTREE
LEES
OLD GUARD

GLENGARRY (MACDONALDS)
KEPPOCH (MACDONALDS)
PERTH & MACGREGOR
APPIN (STUARTS)
LOCHIEL (CAMERONS)

ATHOLL MEN
STRUAN (ROBERTSON)
MACDONALDS OF GLENCOE
MACLACKLANS

LORD GEORGE MURRAY - DUKE OF PERTH

1ST POSITION OF JACOBITE ARMY

SETON
SETON HOUSE
BRIDGE

PRESTON TOWER
PRESTON HOUSE ESTATE
HIGH WALL

1ST AND 3RD POSITION OF ROYAL ARMY

COLONEL WHITNEY'S DRAGOONS
COLONEL GARDINER'S DRAGOONS
PRESTON
2ND POSITION OF ROYAL ARMY
ARTILLERY GUARD
ARTILLERY
IMPASSABLE

MEADOW MILL
DITCH

MARSHY GROUND

RIGGONHEAD DEFILE

BANKTON HOUSE

MANSE
TRANENT CHURCH
TRANENT

LORD STRATHALLAN'S DRAGOONS

RIGGONHEAD FARM

panel 72

TEMPORARY FATE AT LEAST OF SCOTLAND APPEARED TO DEPEND. "WAVERLEY" SIR WALTER SCOTT

MAP OF THE BATTLE

73   The Highlanders line up for battle with the sun rising behind them and some offer a prayer – September 21st

The order of march had placed the Duke of Perth to the north, on the right flank, and Lord George Murray's column to the south as left flank. The MacDonald's under Perth had marched farther than planned to the northwest as Murray had halted. This had the advantage that Perth now outflanked the redcoat line to the north by some 100 yards, but it left a gap in the centre of the Highland line across which the Reserve including the Prince now stood, some fifty or more yards to the east of the other two columns. History tells that many of the Highlanders paused at this moment for prayer.

panel
73

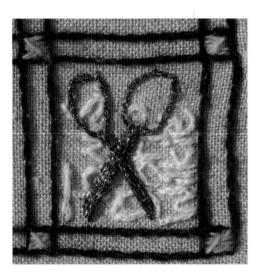

This panel was tramlined by Judith Abbott of Dunblane and then embroidered by Dorie Wilkie, Lead Stitcher for the tapestry. Dorie collected the panel on 9th June and it was completed June 29th with much support from husband Tom. 'I saw rather more World Cup football and Wimbledon tennis than I intended! There wasn't much problem solving needed about plaids as I benefitted from having seen other stitchers exploring ideas for kilts though I do now realize how tricky it was. So it was just a case of getting into automatic needle mode! This was an interesting design and quite different from my earlier panel #19 and I truthfully enjoyed the unexpected challenge'.

6.00 AM

THE SUN ROSE DISPELLED THE MIST AND SHOWED THE ARMIES TO ONE ANOTHER. HOMER

HIGHLANDERS LINE UP FOR BATTLE AND SOME PRAY

The Highlanders line up for battle with the sun rising behind them and some offer a prayer – September 21st

74   Highlanders charge with fierce shouts – September 21st

The Camerons, three ranks deep, were the first to charge veering to their left in order to close the gap between themselves and the ditches thereby preventing any dragoons taking them in their flank. As the sun rose further and the early morning mist dispersed the redcoats saw the Highlanders charging towards them, *'wildly uttering hideous cries, their feet rustling audibly against the stubble of the recently harvested cornfield'.* Then the MacDonalds on the right flank charged too, again veering left but still outflanking the redcoats.

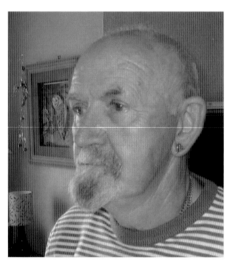
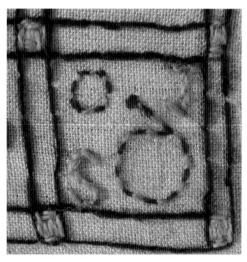

This panel was embroidered by Micheál O Dalaigh from Dublin, father-in-law to the Tapestry's artist Andrew Crummy. 'I had been taught to sow by the nuns who cared for me when I had TB in my knee aged 6, and by age 10 I'd darned 400 dozen pairs of socks, knitted two hundredweight of scarves and patchworked enough blankets to .... but could I sew a tapestry panel?' Michal resolved to find out as he was convalescing after a knee operation. Since his mother's name was Christina Highland, the Highland Charge was the challenge he took up, with Stuart Jones 'keeping him right' – which he clearly did!.

"SEVERAL BODIES; WHERE OF THAT UPON THE LEFT WE JUDGED TO BE AT LEAST 20 IN FRONT AND 30 IN DEPTH" COPE

THE HIGHLAND CHARGE

Highlanders charge with fierce shouts – September 21st

75 Redcoat Officers fire their artillery once as the cannoniers flee – September 21st

As the Highlanders began their charge from their left flank, all the redcoat cannoniers panicked and fled taking all the powder with them. The two redcoat officers who stayed at their posts, Colonel Whitefoord and Master Gunner Griffiths, fired all the available artillery field pieces just once. They had six 1.5 pounder cannons, one of which failed to fire, four coehorns and two Royals. As they fired in amongst the Camerons their charge faltered for just a moment. The redcoat foot soldiers gave a great cheer. But Lochiel urged them on and they soon continued with fierce shouts.

panel 75

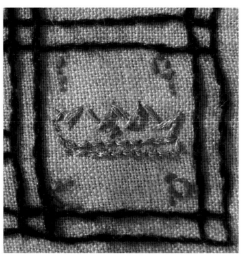

This panel was created by Christina Philp, a Panner born in Crown Square and educated at Cockenzie School which today includes Andrew Crummy's studio where the tapestry was created and the drop-in stitchers' workshops have been held. Embroidery came as a new skill to Christine who has knitted, sewn and quilted much of her life.

WHITEFOORD

GRIFFITH

REDCOAT OFFICERS FIRE ONCE AS THE CANNONIERS FLEE

76 Local people and visitors watch the battle from Preston Tower – September 21st

The battle had been widely anticipated to occur that day but many who had hoped to watch missed the entire engagement since it took place so early in the morning and was of such short duration. Nonetheless many visitors, even from across the Forth, climbed the semi-derelict Preston Tower, destroyed by the Duke of Somerset before the Battle of Pinkie in 1547, to get a fine view. They included the Horsbrugh family who later in the day rescued a redcoat and carried him back to Pittenweem. The local Prestonpans Minister's son, Alexander Carlyle, was awoken in Prestonpans by the gunfire but the battle was over before he was dressed to see it.

This panel was embroidered by Isla Butler of Gullane yet she has a fine Pans pedigree with Burgh Councillor & JP Jimmy Malcolm as an ancestor and Uncle Alex who worked in the Links pit often in 6" of water under the Forth. Isla herself and cousins Robert and Jim Donaldson were accomplished tin tray sliders on the Battle Bing. Embroidery? 'Well of course I had to volunteer, and the enthusiasm and camaraderie has been wonderful to enjoy. In particular I want to acknowledge the kind help given to me whilst I was in hospital by Sandra Wight, Rita Wilson and Hilary Williams.

LOCAL PEOPLE AND VISITORS WATCH THE BATTLE FROM PRESTON TOWER

77   The Camerons capture all the redcoat artillery – September 21st

The Camerons' charge soon brought them to the redcoat cannons, coehorns and royals which had been unable to reload. All cannoniers save the two redcoat officers, Colonel Whiteford and Master Gunner Griffiths, who had fired the available artillery field pieces, had fled immediately the Highland charge began – taking the powder with them. The Highlanders were delighted to have captured such field pieces. They had proved convincingly that they could overcome their traditional dread of artillery.

panel 77

This panel was embroidered by Norma Callison of Fort William since 1976 although born in Fife. Norma's daughter Karen Lees, Daphne Stewart and Johan Morton were recruited to help although none had any experience of embroidering with wool on linen. Norma's 90 year old aunt had taught her to knit and sew as a child. Appropriately stitching took place on holiday at Castle Douglas and in the Glen Nevis sunshine, at the foot of the 'Ben' – which is the tag they all chose!

THEIR FEET RUSTLED AUDIBLY AGAINST THE STUBBLE OF THE RECENTLY HARVESTED CORN WHITEFOORD

WITH A SWIFTNESS NOT TO BE CONCEIVED ELCHO

CAMERONS CHARGE AND CAPTURE THE CANNONS

THEY UTTERED 'HIDEOUS' CRIES

ELCHO

78   Redcoat dragoons falter and turn to flee – September 21st

The redcoat dragoons had been placed behind the foot soldiers and at first moved effectively with a squadron of Hamilton's blocking a small incursion by the MacDonalds on the extreme right flank towards the Forth. That was the dragoons only action however. Elsewhere Whitney's dragoons were in an immediate state of panic and began fleeing from the rear of the lines their horses blocking any chance of moving the artillery to their left flank, as Cope had ordered, when he saw himself outflanked there.

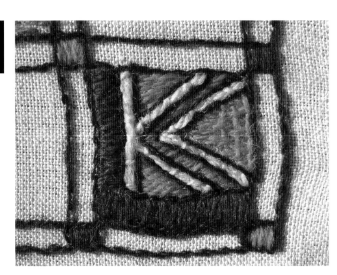

panel
78

This panel was embroidered by Kirstie Collam of Edinburgh. After graduating from Edinburgh College of Art in Dress Design and Embroidery Kirstie worked in theatres across Scotland in wardrobe departments before joining the BBC in Glasgow as a Costume Designer. She returned to Edinburgh as a freelancer in tv as well as embroidering and exhibiting with groups. She was a Visiting Lecturer at Queen Margaret College before becoming Sales Agent for several Art Societies including the RSA, RSW & SAAC. A member of the Costume Society of Scotland she has also worked in antiques and at Jenners – when it *was* Jenners!

COLONEL WHITNEY

DRAGOONS FALTER AND TURN TO FLEE

Redcoat dragoons falter and turn to flee – September 21st

79 Redcoat soldiers fire once but have no time to reload – September 21st

The redcoats facing the Camerons' charge saw it separate into three columns as it reached them. The Highlanders having discharged their muskets threw them down to draw their broadswords and Lochaber axes. The redcoats themselves initially returned the musket fire but had no chance to reload before the Highlanders were upon them. On the redcoats left flank, such had been the fear created already by the Camerons' charge that the foot soldiers turned to flee when the

MacDonalds were still some 60 yards away, without firing at all. There was one small pocket of resistance by a score of foot soldiers led by Colonel Halkett in the grounds of Bankton House but, without putting up a fight, he was persuaded to surrender by Lord George Murray who had much superior numbers – much to Murray's satisfaction since unnecessary bloodshed was avoided.

 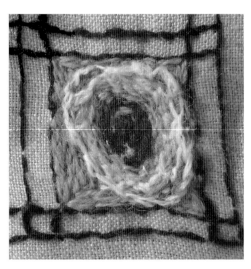 

This panel was embroidered by Anne Dickson, Liz Neilson and Lynn Fraser, who also created #83. Despite travelling every day close by the battlefield Liz knew very little about it. School lessons were a dim memory and there is very little at the site to commemorate it. Indeed how certain were we until recently of the precise location? But the future's bright! 'Our tapestry means we can all know more of our local history and its national significance' – and Liz's grandchildren added a few stitches to the panel. One day they will be telling their own grandchildren about those long ago September events.

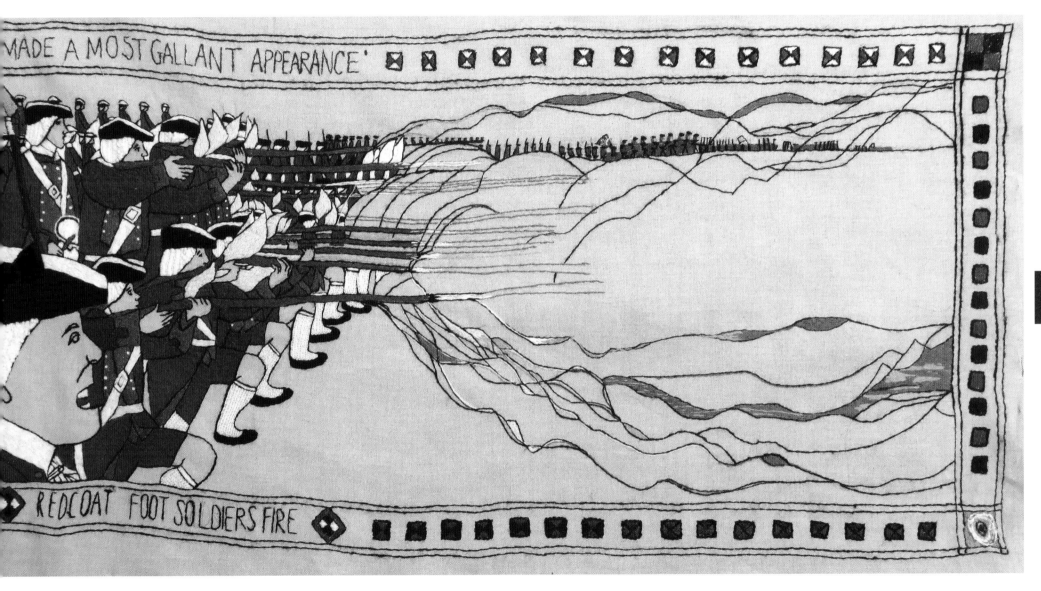

'MADE A MOST GALLANT APPEARANCE'

REDCOAT FOOT SOLDIERS FIRE

80   Redcoat foot soldiers turn and flee – September 21st

The foot soldiers had fired their muskets as the Highlanders charged but had no chance to reload. Around them they saw the dragoons wheeling, escaping, unwilling to attack the enemy. The cries of the Highlanders were terrifying. So the redcoats turned and fled despite the urgings of their officers to stand and fight.

This panel was embroidered by Sarah D McCabe [nee Conachan], a Panner born and bred. 'Grandfather John (the Auld Grinder) played accordion and his sons were all musicians – my father James, Robin and Hugh formed "The Georgians" and played the Empress Ballroom Dalkeith. Educated at Cuthill and St Martin's Tranent, my passion for history saw me at the 2009 Cuthill Battle re-enactments where Elizabeth Jones enthused about the tapestry although when I saw the challenge I very nearly ran away! Yet my panel's image of redcoats running for their lives chased out of The Pans by a hoard of angry Highlanders appealed to my sense of humour. I 'volunteered' although I had never attempted embroidery before. I have been astounded by the patient sharing of skills, not least from Elizabeth, and the camaraderie which has been such a pleasure to experience. Finally, my husband Bill's loving support has been outstanding.

'FOR SHAME GENTLEMEN, DON'T LET US BE BEAT BY SUCH A BAND OF BANDITTI' COPE

REDCOATS TURN AND FLEE

81 The dragoons gather before Preston House and Bankton House in confusion – September 21st

The dragoons fled backwards to the area between the rear of the redcoat foot soldiers and the walls of Preston House with Bankton House to the south. The only way off the field for them was through narrow defiles between the walls of both houses. Colonel Gardiner and others sought to persuade them to return but without success. Confusion and panic reigned with horses rearing up and dragoons thrown from their mounts as they struggled to make their way through the gaps.

This panel was embroidered by Mary Clements originally from County Tyrone in Northern Ireland. Her interest in embroidery was first aroused by a free pattern from The People's Friend, a Scottish Women's magazine – to create a linen tray cloth with thistles, roses, a shamrock and daffodils. More tray cloths, cushion covers, tea cosies and pictures followed. Most recently Mary helped complete a centenary wall hanging for Chalmers Church. Working on her panel has taught her a good deal of Prestonpans history but there have been nervous moments – so many horses!

EARL OF HOME.
EARL OF LOUDON

DRAGOONS ASSEMBLE BEFORE PRESTON HOUSE AND BANKTON HOUSE IN CONFUSION

82 Dragoons flee towards Birslie Brae – September 21st

Those dragoons able to make their way through the gaps between and in the walls of Preston and Bankton Houses paused momentarily to the south west of Preston where Lord Home, pointing his pistol in the air, Lord Loudon and others twice attempted to rally them. But it was to no avail and they took the pathway across the marshy ground up towards Birslie Brae. Yet further attempts to get them to return to the field and take their revenge were fruitless. The chaos created by the Highland charge using Lochabar axes, broadswords and scythes attached to long poles to unseat the dragoons had completely terrified them. There was no appetite at all for a fight.

panel
82

This panel was embroidered by Marilyn Nicholson, a local textile artist who was influenced in stitch from a very early age seeing the beautiful embroidery of her mother, grandmother and aunts. After her daughter 'fled the nest' Marilyn took local classes and eventually gained City & Guilds in Embroidery & Design. She now attends workshops and conferences and teaches textile art locally, where she is a Past President of the local Embroiderers' Guild. Her 7 year old grandson Tristan has become very interested in the whole project and is very proud of the role his Grandma is playing in such a prestigious tapestry of such a famous local event.

THE WHOLE PROSPECT WAS FILLED WITH RUNAWAYS AND HIGHLANDERS PURSUING THEM. CARLYLE

DRAGOONS FLEE TOWARDS BIRSLIE BRAE

83 Redcoat Foot Soldiers are slaughtered at the walls of Preston House – September 21st

Whilst Cope's decision to position his army in the fields close by Preston House meant the Highlanders could only attack from the east. The high walls of the house meant that the redcoat soldiers in flight were unable to escape any further. Many turned their coats in surrender but those that did not were mercilessly slaughtered by the charging Highlanders. With the dragoons blocking the road in their flight, the infantry was completely helpless and rounded up in great numbers. The wounds inflicted were dreadful, and the field was choked with the bitter and bloody evidence of defeat.

panel 83

 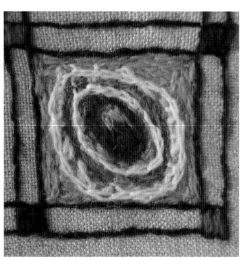 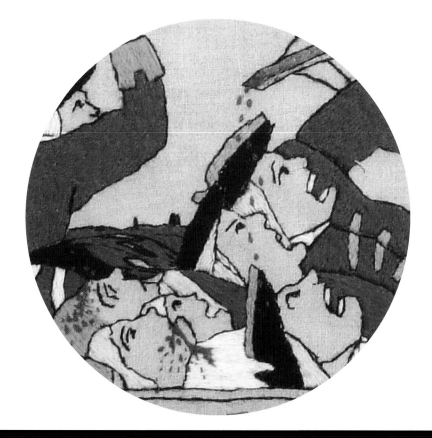

This panel was embroidered by Liz Neilson, Ann Dickson & Lynn Fraser. Lord Grange who lived in Preston House notoriously kidnapped his wife and sent her to St Kilda. She not only knew of his Jacobite sympathies which she could betray, but also of his delight in the Pandores 'Oyster Girls' – young lassies who delivered the oysters for his riotous parties and stayed on to share in the fun – whether they wanted to or not. The oyster tag with three pearls honours those girls. The colours of the wall are taken from local stone, and the blood of the redcoats soldiers and Jacobite warriors runs figuratively across the panel – as does the blood of the apprentice-stitcher Lynn from her numerous self-inflicted stabbings whilst at work on the tapestry.

A SPECTACLE OF HORROR..... WITH HEADS, LEGS AND ARMS, AND MUTILATED BODIES. Johnson

REDCOAT FOOT SOLDIERS ARE SLAUGHTERED AT WALLS OF PRESTON HOUSE

Redcoat Foot Soldiers are slaughtered at the walls of Preston House – September 21st

84 Colonel Gardiner makes a last stand with 17 redcoats – September 21st

Colonel Gardiner knew the land well for he lived in Bankton House and had no mind to flee. He rode to and fro across the crumbling lines and gathered together a small detachment of redcoat soldiers. Cope too sought to rally his army crying: *'For shame Gentlemen. Don't let us be beat by such a set of banditti..... Behave like Britons. Give them another fire and you'll make them run.'* As Cope went off to persuade the dragoons to return to the field, Colonel Gardiner was left alone attempting to stem the rout.

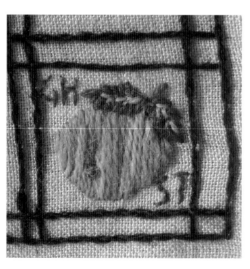

This panel was embroidered by Gloria Holly and Susan Thebeau of Orlando, Florida, USA both of whom have Scottish ancestry. Their involvement with the tapestry arose from Shona Brash Robertson's student ambassadorship from Prestonpans Rotary in 1979 and Gloria's son Chip's return amassadorship to Tranent to stay with James Forrest's family. Their friendship grew and endured but to embroider this panel Gloria enlisted Susan's support as an experienced cross stitcher.

Colonel Gardiner makes a last stand with 17 redcoats – September 21st

85   Colonel Gardiner falls beneath a thorntree – September 21st

Colonel Gardiner's efforts to rally the foot soldiers were in vain. He was eventually wounded by two musket balls and pulled from his horse by a Highlander's scythe under a thorntree on the southern edge of the battlefield, close by the walls of Preston House. The Highlanders then set upon him, and those few who followed him, with swords and lochaber axes. Seeing Gardiner could not rise again his followers lay down their arms. Around them the entire government army had now succumbed. But Gardiner's heroic last stand would be long remembered, not least by the community where he lived. [In 1853 an obelisk to his gallantry and memory was erected by public subscription.]

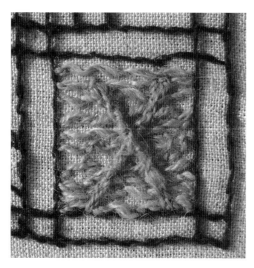

This panel was embroidered by Carmel Daly of Cockenzie. When Andrew Crummy asked if I wanted to stitch a panel I immediately replied: "Yes, but it has to be the thorntree scene". I just knew his tree would be a dark and twisted reality; one suited to my knotty, tangled, twisted way of sewing. And I knew being the artist's wife would mean being one of the last to get their linen and wools! By the time I was just half way through another fantastic community project was under way – coastal rowing. For me and several fellow stitchers/rowers the two became entwined. "Night after night while I stitch I think of rowing our wee 'boatie blest' but while out on the water I heard the cox shout 'IN, IN, IN' as I guiltily thought of all the little stitches I could be laying down. 'Tis nearly done, harbour in sight! "

COLONEL GARDINER FALLS BENEATH THE THORNTREE

86 Colonel Gardiner is carried on a cart to Tranent Manse – September 21st

Colonel Gardiner's manservant, dressed in disguise as a miller, saw his master fall and made haste to arrange for him to be carried away from the battlefield on a cart to Bankton House and from there to Tranent Manse. Gardiner was mortally wounded. As he was carried away it was clear that nothing could now be done that might rally the redcoat army.

This panel was embroidered by Bettine Robertson who taught herself embroidery with kits bought at Jenners and her artwork framed by her husband for presents. A 'senior' octogenarian, she thought she might not be able to meet the challenge of her panel but with the ever present encouragement, plus some supporting kit, provided by the family the result is clear to see. Outstanding work!

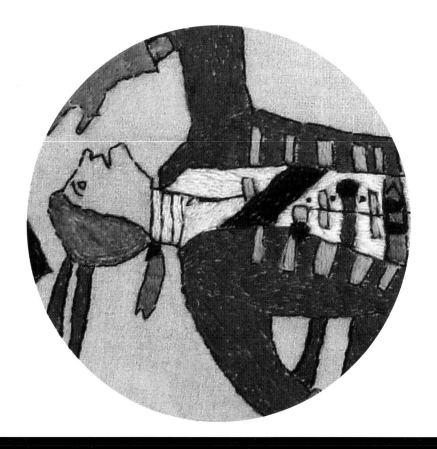

TRANENT MANSE

BANKTON HOUSE

COLONEL GARDINER CARRIED TO TRANENT MANSE

87 Cockenzie House surrenders and Cope's Baggage Train is captured – September 21st

A detachment of Camerons was now despatched to take Cockenzie House where Cope's own baggage train and his personal coach had been left. They were well guarded by kilted government troops of the Black Watch. Nevertheless they surrendered after firing just a single shot on the urging of redcoat Colonel Halkett who, after his own surrender at Bankton House, had gone along with the Camerons. Lord George Murray had by then convinced Colonel Halkett that fighting on was pointless. The capture of Cockenzie House gave the Prince much needed arms and ammunition and several thousand pounds in gold and silver specie. *[Cockenzie House still stands in 2010 next door to the studio where this tapestry was designed by Andrew Crummy.]*

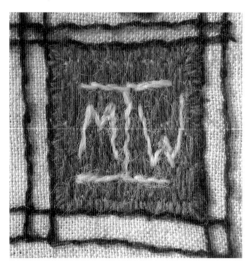

This panel was embroidered by Isabel Weaver, born a Macmillan. She returned to Scotland in the Year of The Homecoming and is now staying in East Lothian. She spent much of her working life south of the Border, on the Isle of Wight in particular, in Higher Education as well as organising recreational activities that included craftwork. Her husband's clan, the MacFarlanes, also came out for the Prince so she had fine home support as she completed her embroidery.

COCKENZIE HOUSE SURRENDERS AND COPE'S BAGGAGE IS CAPTURED

88 Sir John Cope and his Brigadiers flee the battlefield – September 21st

Seeing that his defeat was total, and that only those on horseback could escape, Cope too resolved to flee, making his way towards Birslie Brae in the wake of his fleeing dragoons. It was not an orderly withdrawal but the alternative of making their way to Edinburgh to join General Guest in the castle was deemed unfeasible. The dispirited remnants of Cope's army paused briefly in Lauder and spent the night at Coldstream. Brigadier Fowke, unable to rejoin the fleeing dragoons perforce made his way to the north then east, escaping towards Longniddry. Whilst at Coldstream Cope wrote to Lord Tweeddale reporting that *the men had been taken with a most destructive pannick.*

This panel was embroidered by Lysbeth Wilson of Dunblane. Her mother and grandmother were both excellent needlwomen so from a very early age Lysbeth learnt sewing and knitting. A City & Guilds graduate in Embroidery and Design she loves experimenting with different threads and fabrics and combining differing styles of embroidery. She is a longstanding member of the Embroiderers Guild and keen supporter of the Scottish WI Rurals.

SIR JOHN COPE AND HIS BRIGADIERS FLEE THE BATTLEFIELD

89 The Prince calls a halt to the battle and insists all prisoners must be helped – September 21st

The Reserve line of the Highlanders in which the Prince had stood made no contact with the redcoat army at any time. As he came forward the Prince could see that Victory was his and called for all attacks to cease. He was determined that 'all his father's subjects' should be treated alike and insisted that the redcoat wounded as well as his own wounded Highlanders should be cared for. Cope's officers who were taken prisoner received good care, and medical treatments were provided at Bankton and Preston Houses as well as Prestoun Grange and Dolphinstoun Farm.

This panel was embroidered by Mary Richardson, originally from Eyemouth but now staying in Tranent. On retirement from banking she began craft work and took up her panel to bring back her schoolday embroidery skills. As she worked her friends and family took an increasing interest in both her creation and the whole Tapestry. She wrote and recited the first poem honouring the Tapestry's stitching on March 24th 2010.

THE PRINCE CALLS A HALT TO THE BATTLE AND INSISTS ALL PRISONERS MUST BE HELPED

The Prince calls a halt to the battle and insists all prisoners must be helped – September 21st

90 Colonel Gardiner is nursed at Tranent Manse whilst Highlanders dine unaware in the kitchen below – September 21st

Colonel Gardiner was taken to an upstairs bedroom on his arrival at Tranent Manse and nursed there by Beatrix Jenkinson who only two days before had met the Prince at Duddingston. Later in the morning a party of Highlanders arrived at the Manse in search of redcoats but they were distracted by Mary Jenkinson who served them lamb from the spit in the kitchen below. The Colonel died of his many wounds just before midday and was subsequently buried in the churchyard.

[During late 18th century reconstruction of Tranent church his remains were moved to its interior, a few yards west of the pulpit.]

 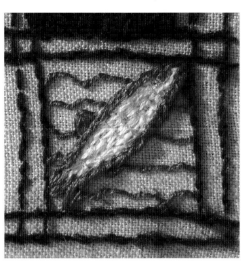

Rhona MacKenzie from Longniddry, East Lothian invited her sister, Catherine Morrison from Denny, Stirlingshire and niece, Rhona Morrison from Glasgow to join her in stitching this panel. This involved travel to and fro but resulted in several lunches and much chat. Catherine and Rhona MacKenzie were born and brought up in Stornoway on Lewis hence the herring as the personal tag. The herring on the town's civic shield carries the motto – 'God's providence is our inheritance'. The herring industry brought great prosperity to Stornoway in the early 20th century. We hope that this Tapestry will do the same for Prestonpans.

21ST SEPTEMBER

FOR KING, AND LAWS, AND COUNTRY'S CAUSE, IN HONOUR'S BED HE LAY

COLONEL GARDINER NURSED BY BEATRIX JENKINSON AT TRANENT MANSE WHILST HIGHLANDERS DINE IN KITCHEN

Colonel Gardiner is nursed at Tranent Manse whilst Highlanders dine unaware in the kitchen below – September 21st

91 All the wounded are tended at Bankton House and other great houses – September 21st/22nd

There were several large houses close to the field of battle to which the wounded from both sides, at the insistence of the Prince and Lord George Murray, were taken. Doctors were summoned from Edinburgh to attend them. Many were taken to Bankton House and Preston House and farther afield to Prestoun Grange and Dolphinstoun Farm. Many redcoats were very severely wounded, often losing limbs in the carnage that the Highlander charge and hand to hand combat with Lochabar axes and broadswords had inflicted on them. There were far fewer Highlander casualties, almost all of whom had gunshot wounds.

This panel was embroidered by Helen Johnstone of Port Seton & Cockenzie. "My interest in sewing was from an early age watching my grandmother who was a seamstress. She taught me how to cut out, machine, knit and embroider. Later I did cross stitch but never a major embroidery." After retirement Helen worked as a community volunteer helping with Christmas lights and then joined the town's famous 'In Bloom' Group which remains her major interest – although "there's still time for sewing and I've enjoyed playing my part in this great project."

CHARLES PROVIDED 'FOR THE RELIEF OF THE WOUNDED OF BOTH ARMIES'.

EVERY APPEARANCE OF MODERATION AND HUMANITY

AS SOON AS THE PURSUIT BEGAN ALL THE PRINCIPAL OFFICERS MOUNTED ON HORSEBACK IN ORDER TO SAVE AND PROTECT GEN. COPE'S OFFICERS AS MUCH AS THEY COULD! ELCHO

THE WOUNDED ARE TENDED AT BANKTON HOUSE

92   The Prince stays overnight at Pinkie House – September 21st/22nd

The Prince spent considerable time ensuring the wounded were taken care of before taking light refreshments with the Chiefs in the open air on a table set up near the captured redcoat cannons. None of the Highlanders had eaten since the previous evening. Afterwards he made his way to Pinkie House to the east of Musselburgh, where he stayed the night. Pinkie House was the home of Lord Tweeddale, the Hanoverian Government's Secretary of State for North Britain – as Scotland was known at that time. Whilst at Pinkie House his Council considered whether they should proceed directly to Berwick-on-Tweed in pursuit of Sir John Cope. They quickly decided against such a course of action, preferring to return to Edinburgh to consolidate their resources including the weapons and ammunition captured from Cope's army.

This panel was embroidered by members of Craft Clinic [further details at #61]. They were naturally drawn to the two panels which depict iconic landmarks in their home town of Musselburgh: ... the Roman Bridge (# 61) and Pinkie House shown here. 'While we were working on this panel at Craft Clinic, we discovered that down the corridor was Sharon Keulemans, who happens to live in Pinkie House and could point out her own bedroom window! We insisted that she stitched the window and in return were given a tour of the house which really brought the story to life for us. In ways like this the tapestry has been more than just a sewing project, but also a surprise and a delight. Stitchers include Gaynor Allen, Jan Dempster, Karen Fiddler, Wilma Harper, Sue Henderson, Sharon Keulemans, Charlotte Kirby, Karyn Malcolm-Smith, Rosemary Taylor and Laura Young. '

The Prince stays overnight at Pinkie House – September 21st/22nd

93 Sir John Cope's carriage is dragged by the Robertsons past Duddingston – September 22nd

The capture of Cockenzie House with Cope's baggage train and personal documents also yielded up his coach. The Robertsons took proud possession of that coach and pulled it back via Duddingston towards Edinburgh and eventually to Straun, carrying their elderly Chief as a passenger much of the way. The coach also contained chocolate drinking paste which was at the time unknown in Scotland but a favourite drink for Cope.

This panel was embroidered by Shona Brash of Port Seton, a Robertson herself who, with her sister Julie Aitken had restored one of the pediment lions on Gardiner's obelisk in Prestonpans in 2007 in memory of their father, an ardent Jacobite. Julie and their mother, Margaret Robertson, also joined in the stitching as did Shona's daughter Nicola.

21ST SEPTEMBER CHOCOLATE TOOTHPASTE

SIR JOHN COPE'S CARRIAGE IS DRAGGED BY ROBERTSONS PAST DUDDINGSTON

Sir John Cope's carriage is dragged by the Robertsons past Duddingston – September 22nd

94 Hundreds of Redcoat prisoners are marched to Edinburgh – September 22nd

The triumphant Highlanders first attended to the wounded and then made their way back to Musselburgh where they camped for the night of September 21st and celebrated in the public houses, Lord Elcho amongst them. They continued to Edinburgh with more than a thousand redcoat prisoners early on September 22nd. Scarcely a hundred foot soldiers escaped to rejoin the garrison in Edinburgh Castle during the night and another hundred made their way into the countryside, most of them eventually arriving at Berwick-on-Tweed.

This panel was embroidered by Rosemary Farmer of Sydney, Australia although she's New Zealand born. Great great grandfather William Hay emigrated there from Edinburgh via Australia's goldfields. An avid embroiderer she heard of the tapestry while visiting her daughter in Musselburgh and volunteered at once. At the age of 6 her love of needlearts began when her grandmother taught her to knit. She dedicates this panel to her Scottish grandchildren Samuel, Benjamin and Daniel Hunter.

HUNDREDS OF REDCOATS ARE MARCHED TO EDINBURGH

RCF

Hundreds of Redcoat prisoners are marched to Edinburgh – September 22nd

95 Sir John Cope arrives at Berwick to confirm his own defeat at Prestonpans – September 22nd

After their overnight stop at Coldstream, the dragoons and Sir John Cope made haste to reach Berwick-on-Tweed to confirm to Lord Ker that his army had been routed at Prestonpans and that Scotland was lost to the Prince. Ker had already learnt of the defeat the previous evening and little was discussed as the dragoons were sent to quarters. Lord Tweeddale's bitter verdict on the dragoons' performance in the sorry affair was: *'they have no excuse but that they are from Ireland!'*

[The design of this panel comes directly from the famous cartoon published in 1745 which inspired the artistic styling of this tapestry.]

This panel was embroidered by Kate Edmunds, confessed spinning and weaving wool junkie, who is a Welsh incomer hereabouts. She resolved to long stitch couch her 'Mr C' on New Year's Eve/ Day 2009/ 2010 and her French knots are cracking little beauties. As for her portcullis, she timed that at 14 hours. With such prose, no surprise her tag is text speak K8!

Sir John Cope arrives at Berwick to confirm his own defeat at Prestonpans – September 22nd

96 The Prince returns to Holyrood Palace – September 22nd

The following morning, September 22nd, the Prince re-crossed the ancient Roman Bridge over the Esk in Musselburgh en route to Holyrood at the head of 800 Highlanders. His pipers joyfully played: *When the King Enjoys his own Again*. The news of the Prince's success spread rapidly and convinced many hitherto uncommitted parties across Scotland and in France to join the Rising.

This panel was embroidered by Thelma Greig and Aileen Buchanan of Kircaldy who have been sewing together since 1989 when they helped create the Dysart Tapestry telling that village's history. Aileen began needle work with a girl's magazine sampler commemorating the Coronation in 1953. Thelma is a skilled needlewoman with City and Guilds. Recently they have worked with Kirkcaldy Museum and Art Gallery undertaking varied tasks including replica costumes from Medieval pilgrims to Victorian ladies and working with professional conservators on early 18/19 century samplers. Working on the Prestonpans Tapestry was fun and enjoyable, not only for Thelma and Aileen but for family and friends who saw the progress and now feel a personal interest in it all.

"WHEN THE KING ENJOYS HIS OWN AGAIN"

THE PRINCE RETURNS TO HOLYROOD PALACE

97 There is much rejoicing in the streets of Edinburgh – September 22nd

The Prince ordered that there be no triumphalism about his victory, reminding all concerned that all who fought were his father's people and many lives had been lost. Nevertheless the Jacobite supporters in Edinburgh and along the route to the city could not contain their joy at the Victory and they cheered and celebrated. General Guest's garrison remained in the castle and Lochiel and the Camerons bivouacked in Parliament House to prevent any sorties out.

This panel was embroidered by Marietta Di Ciacca, born and bred in Port Seton as part of the family that made ice cream at the Harbour Cafe from 1940s to 1980s. Her mother, Betty, was born in Prestonpans and Marietta and her husband Nicholas live today in a house called Thorntree – originally named after a fishing boat out of Port Seton Harbour which in its turn was named after the iconic tree on the battlefield under which Colonel Gardiner was mortally wounded. 'This was my first serious attempt at embroidery and I was delighted to have a panel with such a rich array of characters against such a famous backdrop. I feel privileged to have taken the Prince's cause further south than he himself achieved – stitching during my various train journeys to work in London. I give particular thanks to Edna Elliot-McCall for her help in completing this panel and to Laura, Joyce and Janet for their unswerving support'.

Within the image: 22nd SEPTEMBER

HARBOUR TAVERN

THERE IS MUCH REJOICING ON THE STREETS OF EDINBURGH

98　Balls are held at Holyrood throughout October and the Prince dines in public there – September/October

Whilst the Prince's Council met to explore what next steps should be taken letters were sent by the Prince requesting further Highlander clansmen and financial contributions on the assurance that support from France had been promised. The Prince deliberately lived amongst his father's people. He held regular balls at Holyrood to which young ladies of fashion were invited and he dined in public there every day. The city was captivated by the Prince's openness and youthful ambition and the Prince himself was convinced of the invincibility of his Highland army. On occasions the Prince chose to sleep with them in their camp outside the city walls.

This panel was embroidered by Marietta di Ciacca, her second. Personal details are given at #97. 'This panel has particular political rather than personal significance having being stitched during the May 2010 UK General Election campaign. The stitching at the top of the panel was completed during the UK's first ever televised Party Leadership debate, the flowers and lettering at the bottom during the second and the Highlander in the blue coat was stitched while watching live televised coverage of final results. The lady in neutral colours in the centre was stitched while the first Coalition government in 60 years was being formed and the gentleman in green, though stitched before the campaign started, could be seen to represent the first Green Party MP ever returned to Westminster'.

22ⁿᵈ SEPTEMBER - 31ˢᵗ OCTOBER

ROBERT STRANGE
ALLAN RAMSAY

FEW KNOW MY FACE THO' ALL MEN DO MY FAME

THE PRINCE HOLDS COURT IN EDINBURGH

Balls are held at Holyrood throughout October and the Prince dines in public there – September/October

99 Edinburgh Castle fires its cannons to secure food – October 1st

On the 29th September the Prince decided to cease provisioning the Castle garrison and all communication with General Guest was forbidden. There had been frequent redcoat breaches of promises given. The General replied that if this decision were enforced he would cannonade the city. But the Prince did not believe Guest would fire on innocent civilians and he threatened full reprisals if this occurred. General Guest, however, was true to his word and on October 1st fired the cannonade doing considerable damage and causing injuries. On October 2nd the Prince relented authorising a resumption of communications – but by special pass only.

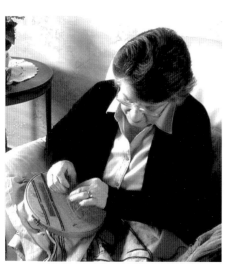

This panel was embroidered by Mary Storrar. An Australian by birth but longtime resident of Dunblane she exchanged suturing for stitching on retirement. As a member of the Culrose needlework group she was involved for the National Trust in creating a replica crewel-embroidered wall hanging for Falkland Palace.

1ST OCTOBER

EDINBURGH CASTLE FIRES ITS CANNON TO SECURE FOOD

Edinburgh Castle fires its cannons to secure food – October 1st

100 The Castle provides specie to the Royal Bank's cashier – October 10th

The resumption of communications with the Castle worked to the advantage of the Prince. On the Highlanders' approach to the city the bankers had sent all their specie to the castle's vaults and were unable to meet the Prince's demands to enable him to fund an expedition into England. However John Campbell, the Chief Cashier of the Royal Bank, was able to gain access with the consent of General Guest who realised that the departure of the Highlanders to England would enable the government forces to regain the capital.

panel 100

This panel was embroidered by Sheila Baird of Aberlady who has deep ancestral roots close to Prestonpans but was born and schooled in England returning to Scotland during The Blitz. Although Sheila has worked on quilting and patchwork for many years she approached this embroidery with some trepidation but found the studio and midway workshops successful motivationally and for skills advice. Genealogical research has happily revealed that the Baron and she are 'cousins' – descended from the parents of golfing Open Winners Mungo and Willie Park Senior.

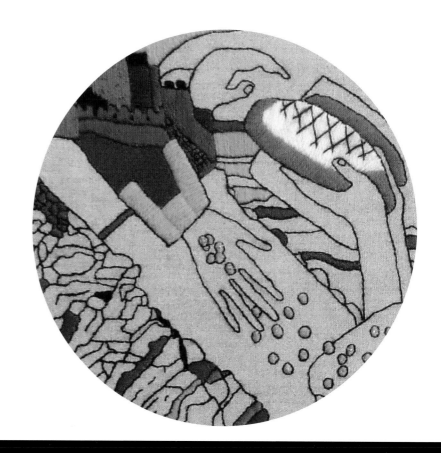

CASTLE PROVIDES SPECIES TO THE ROYAL BANK CASHIER.

101 The Highlanders are trained throughout October in preparation for the battles ahead

Although the Prince had absolute trust in the Highlanders as formidable fighters, Lord George Murray was an experienced military commander. He insisted that the incoming volunteers must be trained and properly equipped with muskets and all that was needed for a long campaign into England such as tents and boots. Two troops of Life Guards were organised and placed under the commands of Lords Elcho and Balmerino. Prince Charles also gave personal attention to the appropriate training of the army, and regular discipline was imposed. The army began losing its exclusively Highland character as recruits arrived in large numbers from the Lowlands and the northeast.

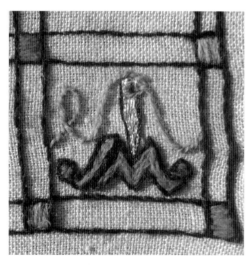

This panel was embroidered by Jacquie McNally, originally from Perth but now of Musselburgh – her second after #37. An experienced costumier, having worked for several years in London, she returned to Scotland with husband Shaun and new born son Charlie in 2002 – he's already inherited his mother's passion for Scottish history and costume design and loves to dress up as a Jacobite. He also helped stitch Arthur's Seat which he's very proud of! Jacquie discovered during the course of stitching this panel that she was born in sight of Arthur's Seat, and her genes include embroidery and sewing – her great grandmother was a milliner and embroiderer, and her aunt has been wardrobe mistress of Perth Rep for many years.

OCTOBER SEE THE BRANDISH BROADSWORD GLANCING

ARTHURS SEAT

HIGHLANDERS ARE TRAINED READY FOR THE BATTLES AHEAD

ROUSE YE ROWS O' KILTED WARRIORS

The Highlanders are trained throughout October in preparation for the battles ahead

102 The Auld Alliance concludes the Treaty of Fontainbleau – October 23rd

With the Prince's Victory at Prestonpans now known in France, the Prince's agent in Paris was able to secure a formal Treaty at Fontainbleau with the French King Louis XV. The French undertook to give assistance and to send troops to defend the provinces that had submitted to the Prince. During the month of October four ships arrived from France with artillery and stores. The Marquis d'Eguilles also arrived in Edinburgh, and Prince Charles appointed him as French Ambassador. For the first time since the Rising began, significant formal military support from the continent seemed probable with his younger brother Prince Henry joining them across the Channel.

panel 102

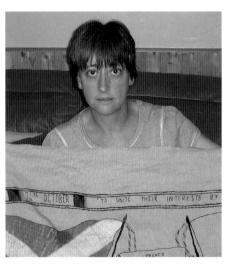
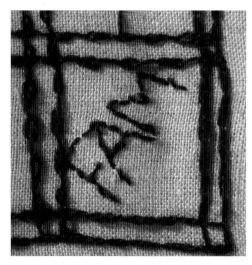

This panel was embroidered by Faith-Ann Mulgrew, who has lived in Prestonpans since early childhood. She works in Edinburgh in the finance section of a large Housing Association, and is actively involved in the community as a Brownie Guider. 'Knowing that my sister Simone was involved with the tapestry [#28] I thought it would be a great challenge to tackle a panel too. I have thoroughly enjoyed sewing it and am proud to have contributed to such a significant project. I very much hope people will enjoy the tapestry for many years to come.'

The Auld Alliance concludes the Treaty of Fontainbleau – October 23rd

103 The Prince's Council debates and agrees to march on London – October 31st

Reinforcements for the Highland army continued to arrive in Edinburgh throughout the month of October including Lord Ogilvy, Gordon of Glenbucket, Lord Pitsligo, Lord Lewis Gordon, the Earl of Kilmarnock and the Duke of Atholl. The Jacobite numbers were now approaching 5000. Meanwhile Hanoverian government soldiers were returning from the continent and

Marshal Wade was making his way towards Newcastle and Berwick. There was intense debate in Holyrood, but the Prince was determined that they must strike into England whilst they still held the initiative and the momentum. It was finally resolved on October 30th/31st that England should be invaded immediately.

This panel was embroidered by Margaret Roberts, Sue Adams & Morag Grant – quilters all. Sue turned down a place at Art College in Bristol but has always had a passion for patchwork and quilting. Margaret and Morag both develped their fascination with sewing, patchwork and quilting from an early age and now offer both formal classes and family tuition to grandchildren.

30TH OCTOBER

LONDON

THE PRINCE'S COUNCIL AGREES TO MARCH TO LONDON

panel
103

104 The Highland Army leaves Edinburgh for England – November 1st

The Highlanders moved out to Dalkeith on the night of October 31st and the Prince slept that night at Pinkie House once again. On the morning of November 1st, although they had all resolved to proceed to Carlisle, the army divided into two columns to confuse the Hanoverian government's spies. The first set out immediately to Peebles and Moffat whilst the Prince proceeded a day later to Lauder and Kelso then, whilst a detachment of cavalry crossed briefly to Woolmer in Northumberland, the Prince turned for Jedburgh. After an overnight stay at Reddings

he crossed Scots Dike to Longtown in England. The entire Highland army met up again at the walls of Carlisle which surrendered after a brief siege on November 15th. The campaign proceeded swiftly and by December 4th the Prince was lodged at Lord Exeter's House in Derby barely 130 miles from London without having faced any further military confrontation since Prestonpans. Swarkestone Bridge across the Trent was taken, and the road to London was open. The three crowns he had promised his father in Rome beckoned.

 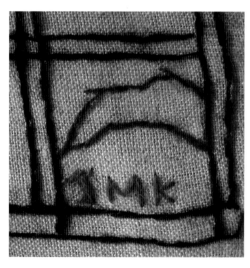 

This panel was embroidered by Joan Kerr of Fort William with much support from her octogenarian mother Elizabeth Carmichael. They both believed the tapestry to be a wonderful project, something to do for Scotland that will live on. It became their winter project when mountain walking was ill advised and gardening not required. In truth it gave them both the greatest enjoyment from working together.

The Highland Army leaves Edinburgh for England – November 1st

Designing the Prestonpans Tapestry

by Andrew Crummy

Creating a 104 metre long tapestry has to be a mad thing to do. But such is the challenge that happens at the Prestoungrange Arts Festival. Over the past 8 years as Convenor of The Prestonpans Murals Trail I have become accustomed to Gordon Prestoungrange's positive creative spirit.

I was trained as an illustrator at Duncan of Jordanstone College of Art, Dundee. I went on to do an MA in Design at Glasgow School of Art. After leaving Art School in 1985 I worked as an illustrator in London for magazines such as *The Observer*, *Time Out* and *New Musical Express*. Around that time I began painting murals for Midland Bank and other large organisations across the world. I would frequently work with large groups to create these artworks. The largest of these murals was a quarter mile long.

I often used history as the basis for my mural designs such as the murals in Middlesborough, Sheffield, around The Scott Monument in Edinburgh and for The National Museums of Scotland. In 2006 I completed a Mural-in-a-Day focussed on the Battle of Prestonpans for the Prestoungrange Arts Festival at the 6th Global Murals Conference which was hosted in the town.

The Prestonpans Tapestry is very much based on the traditions of Community Arts in Scotland with which I have been familiar all my life since my mother was the Organising Secretary of the Craigmillar Festival Society. The aim of any Community Arts project is to produce 'a collective work that will be a catalyst for change'. We all very much hope this fine tapestry will help with the continuing regeneration of Prestonpans and attract many a visitor into the town. When creating an artwork in this particular manner all sorts of possibilities can start to happen. In the following text I aim to show how from a small conversation an artwork can develop and grow.

A contemporary print showing Sir John Cope arriving at Berwick to announce his defeat at Prestonpans, which was the original inspiration for the tapestry.

'I've just been to Bayeux'

One morning in March 2009 Gordon Prestoungrange said to me, at the end of an Arts Festival meeting, in his usual relaxed manner: "I went to see the Bayeux Tapestry last week and I thought we could do that for the Battle of Prestonpans". And after a quick intake of breath added: "but it must be one metre longer, it should be 79 metres overall". At that point I nodded, smiled and agreed with him. From that one brief conversation the journey began.

I headed home and I started telling my wife Carmel Daly about the idea. Well lo and behold Carmel had done a lot of stitching. After 12 years of marriage I discovered a secret my wife had never before disclosed to me!

When visiting the Bayeux Tapestry Gordon had thoughtfully bought a 'kit' which Carmel and I took apart and used to create the first sample of how the Pans Tapestry might look. Almost immediately I took the decision to base the style of the tapestry on the famous cartoon of Johnnie Cope

arriving at Berwick upon Tweed telling of, or rather confirming, his defeat – drawn just after the battle in 1745. I ordered a piece of white linen online and Carmel starting stitching.

I knew next to nothing about stitching. Carmel had been taught embroidery by her father because, when he had TB as a young boy, the nuns in the hospital in Dublin had taught him to stitch. Carmel's father, Michal Dalaigh, I am delighted to tell, has completed one of the panels on the Highland Charge at Prestonpans.

Without Carmel and her knowledge and skill the idea might never have gone anywhere. But on seeing her work we quickly created a series of advertisements and brochures inviting other stitchers to volunteer to help us create the tapestry. The most effective medium was an advertisement on the back of the 3Harbours Arts Festival brochure for June 2009. From that single advertisement our soon to be Lead Stitcher; Dorie Wilkie appeared, and the indefatigable Elma Colvin. I met Elizabeth Jones, another of the indefatigables later that year at the 2009 Battle of Prestonpans Re-enactments in September. I had known Elma for many years because her son Calum had gone to college with me at Dundee.

At this point Gordon began to arrange field visits along the Prince's route initially at his landing point on Eriskay where he recruited several local stitchers. This was followed in August 2009 with a residential week at Borrodale House where the Prince had stayed awaiting the responses of Clan Chiefs 264 years before. We met and recruited many local stitchers as we visited many of the Highland locations associated with the '45. This included volunteers in Arisaig and Kinlochmoidart. It was during this time that we met Sandra Casey in the car park at Glennfinnan, where our resident Bonnie Prince Charlie, Arran Johnson, and his partner Fiona Campbell [dressed as Jenny Cameron] were about to raise the Prince's Standard and rally the Highland Army.

A series of key meetings was also convened amongst all who showed an interest at The Prestoungrange Gothenburg, our arts hub in Prestonpans. To our great surprise, delight and amazement we started getting not just a few but twenty or thirty stitchers coming along. It was at this point in early October 2009 that we began to realise that this mad idea could actually work.

The first sample completed by Carmel Daly based on the 1745 print.

Of Crewel and Wools and Linen

My considerable dilemma, now that we looked likely to have enough volunteers, was I was neither a stitcher nor tapestry expert. I am a trained illustrator/artist/muralist. Which meant I was accustomed to working with a large amount of visual information which has to be drawn or painted. I needed to translate this knowledge into stitch. But what material would I use? Which yarn would I use or was it even yarn? After several visits to New Lanark, where we nearly ended up getting specially made yarn, I knew something was not right. I searched and searched. My problem was I was looking for a design concept to construct the artwork onto.

Then one night I found on the internet an embroidered jacket worn by Bonnie Prince Charlie. It explained it was created in the style of Jacobean Crewel embroidery. A revelation occurred for me, it all fell into place. Then I discovered the Bayeux was done in Crewel work. But where to find crewel yarn? I ordered some online. But the next day my family and I were up town looking at wool shops and a shop assistant asked if we'd been to the Grassmarket Embroidery shop. I entered the shop and there stood a large stand with the beautiful range of Appleton's crewel yarns. Since that moment Sue Black, who owns the shop, has been a very great help throughout the project.

I had found my yarn but what about the linen? I sent away for sample after sample. Eventually I found a Scottish Ecru linen and took it into Sue Black's Embroidery shop where they confirmed it was good – but needed to be heavier. And when Carmel and Dorie both also agreed this was a good way forward we were all set. We had the yarn and the linen. So all we now needed was a finished sample.

Story telling is not illustration of course

I plunged into a world of research, where I immersed myself in any type of visual storytelling that portrayed a battle. I looked at battle paintings, well known movies such as 'Braveheart' and 'Flags of my Father', graphic novels, anything that might give me a clue.

I was readily aware from the outset that I was not illustrating a text with which I was long familiar, rather I was telling a story in stitch. It is a 'traditional' form of public art not widely used today, indeed I was told by someone that it "had definitely gone out of fashion".

The brief was to visualise 79 'event' panels selected by Gordon and derived from the writings of Martin Margulies in his book *The Battle of Prestonpans* published in 2007. Martin's book became my bible. Eventually I would broaden my research to myriad references far and wide including Christopher Duffy's book *The '45* and Stephen Lord's *Walking with Charlie* [Stephen had earlier voluntarily joined us all at Borrodale]. These books have vital visual references but I needed so much more. To make the tapestry work, every element had to have some reference attached to it. There is very little decoration in it that is not taken from an aspect of the period or the Prince's story. In fact, because we recruited many stitchers across the locations the Prince had visited in 1745, such as Blair Castle and Dunblane, there was local knowledge and myth that enabled them to add their own references.

When I was in the depth of creating the work I would be constantly emailing Martin in the USA and Gordon. Arran Johnston became very important and as I emailed Martin he would talk to Arran. As the tapestry progressed Arran became of ever growing significance as he knew what Bonnie Prince Charlie wore and so much more. [Indeed Arran's own book on the Prince, *Valour Does Not Wait*, appears simultaneously with the completion of the tapestry.]

Everything had to be as accurate as possible, but what became apparent was that for each panel there were often two, three or even four versions of the same event – for example how precisely the Prince's Standard was raised at Glenfinnan, and where. Many experts would have different opinions and eye witnesses of the battle would tell it slightly differently. What became unavoidably clear is that the accepted persona of Bonnie Prince Charlie is a concoction of history, myth, fact and romance.

Many of these historical authors would have had firm opinions about the Jacobite cause. There were those who were against and those who were for him. Yet personally I did not want to take sides but rather to try and just 'tell', or rather stitch, this epic tale. As it turns out the story is so full of intrigue, desertion and double agents that it can never be a simple story to tell. My true task was to create visual clarity; to tell the story as clearly as possible.

It is of course a truly epic tale told against the fantastic backdrop of the Scottish landscape and a period of impending change of Scottish culture. It is a story that has inspired many wonderful songs, paintings, poems, dance and literature. My challenge was to translate this into a monumental piece of crewel work.

Searching for a Structure

First I had to find a structure, a way to hang the whole story, a visual language that would tell the story but also be stitched by many people scattered far and wide.

I began by sketching what was in my head, then I reduced each panel to a tiny sketch which was really just a series of shapes related to the story. Next I began to add some detail: houses, mountains, Jacobites, text. Slowly I was building up the references. Through this process I began to realise that parts of the written text would not work as a visual panel, I would have to break them down and tease out the story. It was this teasing out that carried the number of panels from 79 to a final 104.

The next stage was to create the series of panels at A4 size, still very rough working sketches but now with more detail. Some were better drawn than others. These were all to be sent to the local stitchers to verify or add information that I could not or did not know.

Then finally I created the full size drawings that the stitchers would get to work from – each 1000mm x 461mm. These were a big jump in both finish and content. I would first draw out the panel in pencil then use a felt tip marker to indicate the line and filled in area. Even searching out the felt tip markers that made the line to match the yarn was important. It could not be too thick or too thin.

So for months I lived in my studio, not seeing my family, through one of the coldest winters in many years. I created 104 metres of drawings standing half a metre tall. Each night as I walked home I told myself how fast I was going, working out how many I had to produce a day. Being positive all the time. When I had a good day I would praise myself for producing two finished drawings, on a bad day I was telling myself how I would finish off the panel tomorrow morning.

A detail of the sketch for The Canter of Coltbridge panel.

Always positive, always telling myself I would get there. I worked all the way through the Christmas break, taking only Christmas Day and New Year's Day off completely. It was easy starting off; a great feeling at having done 10 drawings, at 20 or 30 the end seemed a long distance away. When I reached 50 drawings it was just wonderful. At 80 drawings the end seemed so near but somehow miles away. Then one day somehow I was at the end!

Drawings to Linen by Light Box & Stitching the Panel

As soon as a drawing was done it was transferred onto linen, at first by Elma Colvin. She had been given, on loan from her son Calum, a large Light Box. I will always be grateful to Elma who traced out nearly fifty panels in her home. By Christmas my friend Pat Fox had made two light boxes for me. Elizabeth Jones, and many others, came and traced the rest of the panels onto the linen.

Finally before Gillian Hart despatched the drawings away to the stitchers Elma and Dorie prepared the linen and the wool and the notes to go with them – all in an elegant tube.

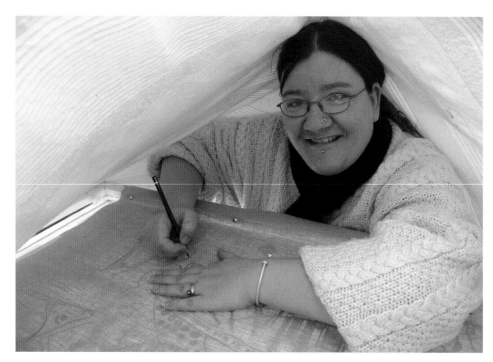

Elizabeth Jones tracing out a panel onto the linen, under blanket on the lightbox.

The first panel to get started was based on the cartoon of Johnny Cope arriving at Berwick upon Tweed confirming his own defeat. And this was given to Kate Edmunds, who has been meticulous in her embroidery. Next came Dorie Wilkie's panel showing Edinburgh baking bread for Johnnie Cope's army.

Once the panels and drawings were out with the stitchers my role changed. We initiated Thursday morning drop-in stitching sessions at my studio. And we started field visits and personal telephone and email contact with those stitchers who could not come to our workshops. A further significant element in all this was that Gordon created an exellent website where pictures of the panels were put up as they progressed. An example of how it worked was when Elma Colvin, who was embroidering 'The Seven Men of Moidart' panel, completed a tartan kilt. That kilt was photographed and widely shared. This inspired others to have a go at doing a tartan. Later on Mary Richardson completed several beautiful embroidered tartan kilts for the 'Prince calls a halt to the Battle' and once again this inspired others. Another inspirational picture circulated was

Esther Sharpley's rendering of trees. Maud Crawford's £30,000 Reward panel was another inspiration.

The Thursday morning drop-in workshops were always well attended. They became motivational mornings where the stitchers brought in their successes and their problems. Every time a panel came in a group of stitchers would stand over it, always curious, always focused. Always eager to learn. Some of the stitchers were very experienced indeed but most had little or no experience. All would devour information and skill. The extent of supportive group learning that has gone on has been truly amazing to me. At the special Mid-Way party we convened more than 70 ladies gathered for a day of sharing and stitching and learning – and the Prince (aka Arran Johnston) inspected their progress.

The 'Second' Story of the Tapestry

I feel very strongly indeed that the 'second' story of our tapestry, one which one imagines the Prince would have greatly enjoyed, is of the army

Stitchers at the mid-way party

of volunteer stitchers. Once again the Raising of the Prince's Standard has worked its magic. His army of stitchers has rallied together to transform my drawings into something truly dynamic. And Cameron of Lochiel, on cue, joined them too to add his stitches!

How can a large and disparate group learn so rapidly? Enormous credit goes to the natural leadership skills of Dorie Wilkie which has seen the stitchers working almost as a single unit. As the tapestry has progressed the stitching has become at once more complex and boldly confident.

My aim was never to produce a series of 'finished' panels, but a sketch that would hopefully encourage stitchers to give each panel the stamp or mark of their own individuality. So the final work is multi-layered as together we do indeed tell the Prince's story. It is a single work of art with a dramatic story line, but deeply layered with human interest and individuality.

I am often asked how I feel when I see one of my drawings so beautifully stitched. There is no easy answer to that question. Time and again I am left speechless. Together we have created a dazzling and unique Scottish work of art stretching 104 metres. The detail in the stitches is truly amazing. Every inch of that length has been stitched by human hand. That is new poetry, the poetry of our tapestry. Into those panels perhaps 10 million stitches, 25,000 hours of embroidery by more than 200 women – and two men. For a whole range of reasons each one agreed to complete a panel for the Prince, for Scotland, for a place in our nation's history. But also it has been my greatest pleasure to know that our volunteers have created their panels for reasons of personal caring and community, the very opposite of the bloody scenes depicted in the final stages of our tapestry at the Battle of Prestonpans itself.

It has been a quite extraordinary journey, one that will continue. Who knows where it will end?

Andrew Crummy drawing out the finished panel "The Prince Offers a Reward of £30,000 for the Elector of Hanover"

Stitching The Prestonpans Tapestry

by Dorie Wilkie

My own awareness that our tapestry was to be created arose from seeing an appeal for volunteer stitchers on the outside rear cover of the 3Harbours 2009 programme. And as my volunteering at the National Trust for Scotland was just coming to an end I felt such a project might be ideal. So I emailed the contact and by return Gordon, the Baron of Prestoungrange responded with a brief message of 'welcome'. Curiosity aroused as I had no idea there was a feudal Baron in Prestonpans but still not hugely convinced this was a serious project, I asked for further information and that was precisely what I received – all the notes from planning meetings, sketch drawings, grand ideas. I was convinced. This was indeed serious and potentially very intriguing!

Prior to my involvement the Baron had commissioned a leading local artist from the Prestoungrange Arts Festival, Andrew Crummy, to 'create a tapestry like that in Bayeux'. His wife Carmel and friend Kate researched wools, and linen in preparation for such an ambitious project. Along with several other lady stitchers, I attended the first meeting at the Prestoungrange Gothenburg in Prestonpans where the Baron enthusiastically gave us a history lesson about the Battle in Prestonpans in 1745, the route the Prince and Cope had taken to that conflict, and an outline of the vision for the panels accompanying regular re-enactments in the future.

The intended outcome for Prestonpans at large was a Living History Centre where tourists, specialist visitors and school parties could come and see the finished work and learn the history it recounted. The Baron had visited Bayeux and bought back a d-i-y embroidery kit which had fired off the original notion. And at this point it is appropriate that I should clarify that what we have created is in fact an 'embroidery' but, like the Bayeux Tapestry, although neither were woven on a loom we've called ours a tapestry too.

Early sketches of most panels had already been drawn by Andrew Crummy and they were laid out for us to choose a panel which might interest us. Reasons for the choices we made varied from being located in an area where someone had personally lived or of which they had ancestral or own fond memories. Or we simply liked the sketch. For example Esther Sharpley's panel is set where she and her late husband camped and walked all around Glenfinnan; and Jacquie McNally's parents were married in the Salutation Inn Perth depicted on her panel. My first choice was a panel with Fife in the background as my husband's family hail from there.

One of Andrew's earliest 'final' sketches – although 'final' as we were all soon to find out was open to further interpretation – was a cityscape of Edinburgh depicting that part of the story when General Sir John Cope, the Prince's adversary in the field, asked Edinburgh to bake bread in a hurry for all his soldiers as they departed into the Highlands shortly after the Prince landed in Eriskay. Andrew Crummy asked that I stitch it as a sample. So, after a successful cataract operation I took it on holiday with me and stitched all the outlines and brought it back to show him. He just looked at it in silence. Nervously I asked him if it was alright, perhaps I had misunderstood what I was to do.........? Finally he observed that he had never seen his work stitched in wool and how very different a drawing on white paper looked when placed on a soft grey coloured linen! Then, fortunately he said he liked it greatly and wanted to use it in the final line-up! This 'sample' over time developed into *my* panel and I had to hand over that Fife panel I had initially coveted to another embroiderer who has made a lovely job of it.

Co-ordinating Ourselves

As time moved on I got to wondering how 'they' were going to co-ordinate the stitchers, keep proper uniformity across the work, determine precise colours, type of wool and linen and the required levels of workmanship.

After offering to help out once too often I was invited to do just that and the grand title of 'chief/lead stitcher' was conferred on me!

From childhood I had drawn and sewn things like dolls clothes, graduating to sewing clothes for myself, commissions for others and selling at craft fairs over the years. After having my two daughters I was able to study for my City and Guild in Embroidery and Design at Telford College in the mid 1980s learning traditional stitchery then making contemporary examples. Later I attended Leith School of Art for several years when it first opened. Along the way I had also trained as a counseller so I felt reasonably confident about filling the role but it was certainly going to be more of a co-ordinating leader than a chief!

It must be said that, although the long standing Arts Festival team were vastly experienced at mobilising volunteers and mounting painting and pottery exhibitions and other varied events, none of them were yet aware how different sewing is in comparison to these mediums especially in the time needed to complete the task. Hand sewing is not a quick thing to do and people vary in the speed and the confidence with which they work. And once the panels are completed the 'end' stitching team has to address the processes of blocking, backing, joining and preparing for exhibition. So I have to confess to some very considerable anxiety for a while both with the plans and expectations they had for a completely different arts discipline and the time scale envisaged. Originally the tapestry was to be finished by 1st September 2010 but that was brought forward to the end

of June 2010. It is to the huge credit of nigh on two hundred volunteer stitchers across the country who have put in hundreds of hours of work to achieve their fantastic panels in record time. We have produced currently the longest 'tapestry' in the world although not the largest, that honour going to the World Tapestry now housed in British Empire and Commonwealth Museum in Bristol which took 23 years to make.

Who were our stitchers?

How did we recruit our wonderful team of stitchers? By the time I came on board the Baron, artist Andrew Crummy and colleagues had already visited Nantes and St Nazaire in France, Eriskay and a host of other locations along the route that Bonnie Prince Charlie took, recruiting stitchers along the way. This initial group plus those brought in like myself via the the 3Harbours publicity continued to grow through local press articles, friends and family and networks spreading the word. We even ended up with a waiting list of people keen to take a panel. This proved valuable as one or two panels were returned where the original stitcher

was not able to complete the panel due to unforeseen circumstances. It was invaluable when Andrew Crummy decided yet another panel was required which he continued to do as late as April 2010. The original remit of 79 x 1000mm x 461mm panels which I initially thought so daunting has eventually ended up with the 104 presented in this book, plus a logo panel and Stitchers' Roll.

Behind every panel there is of course a human story about our volunteers. They range across all ages, (the eldest is Bettine who is 88 years young,) social backgrounds, needlework abilities, full/part time workers – everyone with differing family situations from many locations across Scotland then to Ireland, England, France, the USA and Australia. This has all necessarily influenced their approach to their work as you will discover as you read their biographies on the pages facing their panels. Some had never embroidered before but wanted to be part of the project, or had limited experience having only stitched kits, or had vague memories of making aprons at school. On the other hand we had more than a few very experienced stitchers who had attended various courses, were active

left to right some of our stitchers
Liz Neilson, Anne Dickson, Mary Clements
and Isabel Weaver

makers, and were able to adapt more easily to the freer style of embroidery required for the panels. The more experienced helped others with their expertise at the noisy Thursday morning drop-in sessions we set up for nine months in Andrew Crummy's studio in Cockenzie and in specially convened groups across the country. Sadly we only have one man stitching a whole panel, Michal Dalaigh in Ireland.

For some of our stitchers the project offered them a grand chance to meet new friends and continue in small groups afterwards, for others it has been a therapeutic process after a bereavement, illness or a reason to leave their homes and meet others, a focus for their creativity. We discovered there were many individuals and stitching groups around the various areas who weren't aware of one another but are now. The word I shall always remember being most bandied about over the months was 'addicted' and apart from setting up another project..... I'm not sure how to detox our stitchers. Many husbands and partners have been neglected as we have threaded up and the hours slipped by getting that shield right.

Some have gone to extraordinary lengths to get accurate information about their part in the story e.g. Vennetta Evans wanted to get the moon and stars on the night of September 21st 1745 right for her panel as the Highlanders marched along the Riggonhead Defile. Her search led her to the Astronomer Royal and from him to his French equivalent who actually had the necessary records. Sandra Casey persuaded today's Cameron of Lochiel to add a few stitches to the panel the Fort William Group worked on which was telling of his ancestor's role. Jacquie McNally involved Viscount Strathallan, who commanded the Prince's horsemen. Others spent hours scanning books and paintings for plaids and tartans of the time sharing their ideas.

Early Highland military uniform.

For the Highlanders their clan systems, clothes, colour and weaponry were a mark of distinction among themselves and a contrast to the Lowland Scots. To outsiders they were seen as 'exotic'. There are contemporary pictures held at Windsor Castle of the rank and file Highlanders as they appeared in 1746 painted by Morier for the Duke of Cumberland. A Swiss artist, Morier was commissioned to paint a complete series of the regiments of the British army as well as Royal portraits and his work has always been considered extremely accurate. In the 'Incident of the Scottish

Rebellion 1745' the Highlanders represented were derived from prisoners taken at the time and give a good idea of their dress.[1] John Telfer Dunbar examined the picture and describes their dress in detail. One has his trews being fastened with red garters and black over-lines, in varying thickness and regular pattern his waistcoat darker in pattern, red and black unlike the trews. The jacket has a red background with dark green and white stripes underneath wearing a white shirt and brown undergarment. Blue bonnet, white cockade and black sporran. Others very similar but wearing slightly different woven tartans, wearing a kilt of red with blue and black lines, and light red waistcoat, red, black, and green hose'. Each figure is described in detail all wearing a variety of tartans on their kilts, plaids,

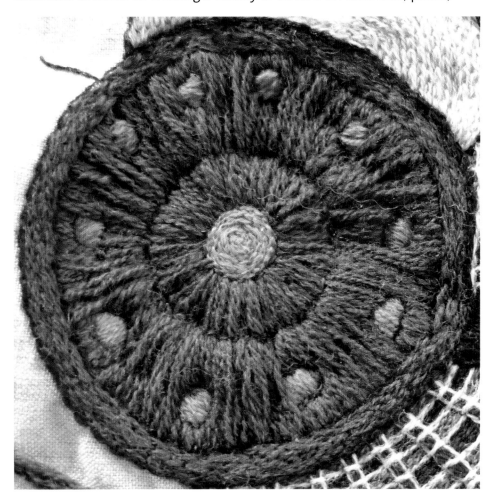

Detail of a shield

trews and hose. They were wielding broadswords, bill-hooks, pistols and holding circular targes with central spikes (half an ell in length). These images and descriptions are a pictorial record of at least 23 tartans worn by eight Highlanders, none of which are recognized by experts as 'clan' tartans.

The Highlander's habit was a belted plaid called *breacan* woven in fine wool or *eileadh* when referring to the pleated long kilt – the Gaelic word for tartan being *breacan*[2] – which was a large piece of tartan cloth approximately 10 x 2 yards. Generally a plaid – Gaelic *plaide* meaning blanket – was woven in one direction and tartan referring to checked or coloured cloth with lines woven in both directions forming a sett.[2] There was no uniformity of 'clan or district ' tartans with symmetrical designs people think of today until the late eighteenth even early nineteenth century. There is no mention by Jacobite bards at the time of 'clan' tartans[3] the tartans referring only to differing colours and patterns (setts), created and varying by the thickness of line in the warp or weft in the weaving.

However 20 years earlier, General Wade in 1725 when employed to demilitarize the Highlands, tried to create some form of uniformity for recruits, by directing his officers to provide plain clothing and bonnets in Highland dress for non-commissioned officers, and the plaid for soldiers of each company to be as near as they can of 'sort and colour'.[1]

The pleated part of the long kilt hung below the waist while the rest of it was pinned at the shoulder with silver, brass or iron, and it doubled as a blanket at night as the winter plaids were extremely warm and in the summer, light and airy. It was suggested this gave the Highlander greater freedom of movement over rocky landscapes, crossing bogs and rivers unlike breeches which would have to be removed to keep them dry to prevent ill health.[4] Apart from being practical and cheap they were classless. This evolved through practicality to the *feileadh beag* (small kilt) phillabeg worn with stockings of the same tartan or plain and coloured garters (sometimes with hay or straw garters). There are however also many references to trews or short hose of wool and tartans which sometimes lengthened into tight trousers or *triubhus*.

A fighting Highlander

Blue bonnets and white cockades

Under their plaids and tartans they wore a belted shirt made of wool or linen called a *lenicroich* or large shirt, some dyed a saffron colour and apparently not washed too frequently. Many Highland men wore a short coat or *cota-goirid* described as closing with gilt clips worn over waistcoats often of different tartans, as well as plain fabrics worn with trews or breeches under the large shirt.[1] Stocks or neckerchiefs were worn not only for fashion or warmth but for some protection against sword blades, while gentlemen wore lace jabots and cuffs representing their status. A 'Short History of the Highland Regiment' published 1743 describes the Highlander 'wearing a sort of thin pump or brogue so light it did not impede his running, or ability to advance or retreat with swiftness. A small leather purse/pouch or sporran with semi-circular brass clasp could hang from the belt sometimes made from badger, goat or seal skins and in certain portraits embellished with designs. The leather was dressed with birch bark and made into goods by each house in smaller communities'.

However it was the Gaelic tradition of wearing a ribbon, rosette or piece of silk on their bonnets that identified friend from foe not their tartans. J. Ray[5] quotes coming upon a young Highlander who stated he was a Campbell, and was asked to identify himself by his bonnet. The Highland bonnet was therefore a very important item of clothing in a man's wardrobe. They were predominantly blue wool, sometimes dark green or dark red, and were not made of tartan. They were usually worn flat on the head and around 1745 were generally at least 12 inches across and decorated as follows:

A white cockade (ribbon or fabric in a bow or rose shape) for Jacobites, worn in front. Red or yellow crosses of cloth or ribbon for the Loyalists.
Clan – a sprig of your Clan's plant badge identified you, worn in front.
Feathers – worn only by chiefs, sub-chiefs, cadets, or senior Clan officials in some clans.
Boss – (the wool pom-pom) rare, possibly occasionally worn by those in military command positions so they can be identified from behind by the men following them.
Metal Clan badges – not worn in the 18th Century[6]

I'll sell my rock, I'll sell my reel,
My rippling-kame and spinning wheel,
To buy my lad a tartan plaid,
A braid sword, durk, and white cockade. **By Robert Burns**

The Highland Army's dress

Prince Charles Edward Stuart adopted Highland dress for 'uniforms' for his army in 1745 and thereafter tartan became a potent symbol for Jacobitism perhaps as a result of a gift of Highland dress from Scottish Jacobites before he arrived in Scotland. A repeated phrase in Jacobite songs of his soldiers describes blue bonnets and tartan plaid, or tartan trews and 'laigh-heeled shoes'.[2] However while a fugitive later in the campaign Hugh McDonald of Baleshare described meeting Prince Charles on Uist wearing borrowed clothes from Lady Clanranald, 'a tartan short coat and vest, a linen nightcap, face and hands with soot drops, a short kilt, tartan hose and brogues, his upper coat of English cloth'.[1] Another recorded story of the time whilst the Prince was a fugitive in the Hebrides was that having been provided with a kilt he leapt in the air saying 'he only required an itch to feel a complete Highlander'![1a] A letter written by an attorney of

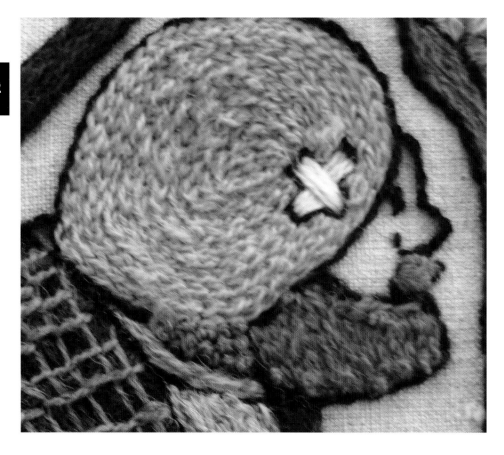

222

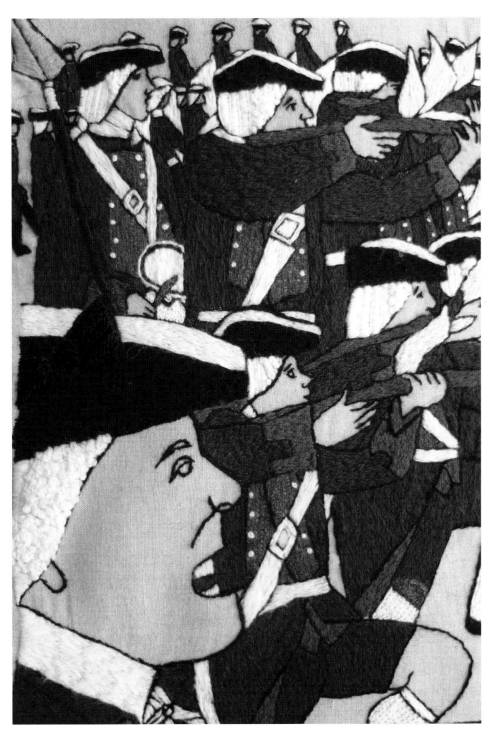

Cope's redcoats

Macclesfield in 1745 describes the Highland army 'walking in regular order' with bagpipes playing instead of drums at the head of each column of their respective regiments. All in Highland dress except 'ye body Guards who wore Blue bound with red. The Prince was in Highland dress with a blue waistcoat bound with silver, a blue cap. He was a very handsome person of a man rather tall, exactly proportioned and walks well'.[1b]

We can see from contemporary portraits what those of status wore, embellishing their tartans with heavy gold lace and ornamented belts and the shirts ruffled with delicate white lace. A description of Alexander MacDonnel of Glengarry returning from France to take part in the Jacobite Rising has him wearing a 'short coat and belted plaid of red and black, richly embroidered with gold and faced with white silk. The waistcoat made of white silk and gold embroidered, with ornamented buttons like those of the coat, richly chased and gilt. The belt is ornamented with silver mountings set with jewels. His attendant/carnach holds the chief's small flat blue bonnet distinguished by the red and white cockade. The attendant is dressed in scarlet cloth 'short coat', waistcoat and a red tartan feile-beag, reckoned to be the first image of the short kilt 1747.'[6] Also Lord George Murray is depicted in a painting in Blair Castle as wearing a blue bonnet with white cockade, belted plaid of green, blue and red tartan the warp only having red. Looking at the paintings sometimes the figure is recorded wearing a combination of several tartans, as well as patterned hose and garters.

The first recorded example of kilt is 1692 and is in the collection of the Scottish Tartans Society. By 1749 the Act of Proscription[7] banned the wearing of tartans, Highland dress, speaking Gaelic and playing bagpipes, except by government troops, but it was repealed in 1785. This ban had perhaps the greatest effect on the evolution Highland dress with Lowland influences, the loss of expertise in weaving and dying during that time all contributing. A Gaelic song in 1746 in praise of Highland dress warned King George of the loss of revenue from customs when there would be a lack of demand for the imported dyestuffs.[8]

Thoughout the panels there is a selection of wigs which were worn at the time by a variety of people on different occasions and treated in a variety of stitches – discussed later. During this time various colours were worn although white was becoming more popular and the curls were getting tighter. Later wigs or the natural hair were worn long, brushed back from

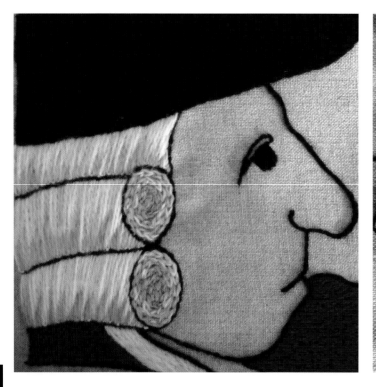
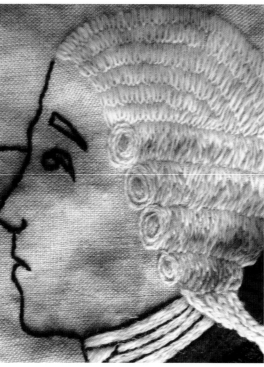

Fabulous wigs!

the forehead and *clubbed* or tied back at the nape of the neck with a black ribbon. A bag wig gathered the back hair in a black silk bag worn by higher social classes.[5]

We don't have too many ladies featured throughout the story but *earasaids* (lady's shawl or horse blanket), or arisaids were commonly worn by women in the Highlands and Islands as an outer or over garment over either a short or long gown with a waistcoat over two petticoats, of stripes or tartan. Some arisaids may be seen in the Highland Folk Museum or Inverness Museum, also one dated 1726 in the Scottish Tartans collection. A plaid consisted of a rectangular piece of finer woollen material two by three yards and sometimes for those of wealth and status, wool lined with silk, or silk for best wear.[8] Described as usually having a white ground with red, yellow and dark green coloured stripes. Depending on status fastened with a silver, iron or brass large buckle with celtic designs and set with stones quite often. A description of the time the *'undress of the ladies'* was the plaid. *'It is made of silk or fine worsted, chequered with various lively colours, two breadths wide, and three yards in length; it is brought over the head, and may hide or discover the face, according to the wearer's fancy or occasion; it reaches to the waist behind; one corner falls as low as the ankle on one side; and the other part, in folds, hangs down from the opposite arm'.[2] ' while around the head was still worn a kerchief of fine linen, closely fitting, with its loose ends tapering down the back. The women of this class went barefoot during the greater part of the year.'* Young girls wore a ribbon around their hair until they were married or had a child when they wore a form of linen cap, *am breid*, white tied on by silk or pinned. Edmund Burt also mentions that women mostly went bare foot but servants were given an allowance for shoes to be worn on Sundays![2]

However, Burt also noted *'Highland women of fashion ... generally well-dressed in the English mode'* when they wore a simple chemise or sark with a striped, plain or unusually tartan petticoat under hooped, open fronted skirts. Or depending how fashionable the circles were that they moved in, corseted bodices with panniers holding the skirts out over the hips. This evolved into sack backed gowns, closed skirts with low necks filled with a lacy fichu, the fullness falling from the box pleats at the back of the neckline into a small train. We have a magnificent example of one such in Marietta di Ciacca's panel 98 as the Prince held Balls at Holyrood Palace.

A fine lady in Palace of Holyroodhouse

Lady Lude

Alan Ramsay painted Flora MacDonald in a white wide sleeved chemise, tied with a pink bow at the elbows; a sky blue sleeveless top over a wide skirt, and a tartan stole fastened around her back shoulders on her right shoulder, with white roses in her hair and bosom (in the Bodleian Library). An early painting of about 1745 shows the daughter of Sir Patrick Murray of Ochtertyre, Helen, wearing a tartan dress with a red background and dark blue, green and black stripes. Her dress is corseted with a stomacher, and the neckline is low with a lace fichu, the three quarter sleeves show her sark underneath edged with deep lace and had a full skirt. She holds a white rose for the Jacobite cause.

Sylvia Robertson and the Robertson stitchers of the Prince's visit to Blair Castle in panel 36 chose to embroider Charlotte Lady Lude's ball gown with violets, showing faithfulness, and primroses for youthful hope of new beginnings.

The designs, materials and stitches

Andrew Crummy has described in the previous chapter how he created the images on each panel and the interactions he had with the embroiderers, which would regularly produce tweaks as the stitching progressed. The images on the panels each measure 1000mm x 461mm and as can readily be seen each panel varies in complexity. Initially, once the panels were designed the future stitcher was asked to sign it off after checking locally all the key details such as the buildings, hill contours, sea in the right place for the area depicted, and then the 'final' drawing was completed.

The 'final drawings', all 104 of them, were then routinely placed on a large light box and traced on to the cut linen lengths. A stitcher's 'kit' of the necessary wools was then assembled with the artist's drawing and the traced linen so that packs in a cardboard tube could be despatched to the volunteers. Sheer volume of panels meant of course that there was a considerable lag between the first and last reaching the individual stitchers. Two got lost in the post and others took longer to travel to France, Ireland Australia and USA. Those last receivers in Spring 2010 who managed to complete their panels on time deserve particular praise.

It then became apparent that it was sometimes a tad overwhelming for volunteers to receive this large piece of linen with the traced image, wools, a few instructions and not much else. More than a few concerns were raised regarding getting the traced lines exactly correct especially where they wore off, following the exact colours and personal interpretation. Not everyone was comfortable to make decisions about techniques or colours without the opportunity of a discussion. So we realised we needed to arrange support remotely by email and phone hotline and/or by arranging visits to groups. Together these two approaches proved effective. Meantime Andrew Crummy also offered his studio for a regular Thursday morning drop in sewing clinic which grew and grew as enthusiastic embroiderers shared their ideas.

The website for the Battle of Prestonpans 1745 Heritage Trust was already up and running so Gordon Prestoungrange created a continuous work-in-progress field there for the embroiderers to access and see phased instructions with images. Firstly, brief stitch suggestions such as stem stitch for the parallel outline on all the panels, filling stitches and contact details for myself and Andrew Crummy were provided. Later we added photographs of worked examples as they were done to inspire others. This again proved much appreciated and invaluable as a reference source especially for the more geographically remote ladies and a great morale booster as we could all see the whole tapestry starting to emerge from the linen and wool kits. The website in due course also became the accessible structured archive for stitcher's completed panels, their biographical details and the history blurbs explaining each of the panels – the critical ingredients for providing a global internet presentation for years to come.

Influences, techniques and light history

Of Colours: The only Highland towns in the eighteenth century where trading of skins for dyes, salt and linens took place were Inverness and Dunkeld, so the woollen cloth had to be spun and dyed locally by the women. The domestic dying of wools occurred for centuries before commercial ventures using many locally grown plants such as ragwort, lichen or larch needles, water lily for blacks. The fixative or mordant used was iron or alum which helped the wool absorb the colours. In Scotland iron was mined and found in black bogs but there is also reference to iron imported to Leith in 1491.

The end results of dying depended on a number of variables such as time of year plants were picked, amount of rain, slow burning peat fires and the quantity dyed at one time. All these elements gave rise to differing shades.

Andrew using a lightbox on Celia Mainlands panel

If no alum was available for example then fir-club moss was used. The fibre of Highland wool was hard and fine and did not take dyes as easily as Lowland wool, so it had to be steeped in dye liquor (stale urine) to prepare it for days or weeks. Foreign trade allowed for difficult colours to be obtained such as madder for reds or Mexican cochineal, woad and indigo imported from Holland as a paste or powder. Dying on different grounds giving shades made them more exclusive and desirable. Scientific analysis of dyes on archival materials, especially fragments attributed to Bonnie Prince Charlie, at the National Museum of Scotland since 1995 has confirmed this.[8] Analine dyes were not introduced until the mid nineteenth century.

Although written in 1689, over half a century before the Prince's campaign, the following description from Grameid[8] gives us an idea of

Top-bottom right details of stitches used for clothing; couching, split, straight and running. Bottom left – all panels were outlined along the pencil lines with black stem stitch

colours worn. 'Glengarry's men were in scarlet hose and plaids crossed with purple stripe ; Cameron chief in his tri-coloured tunic trimmed with gold lace; MacMartin had saffron ribbons and tunic embroidered by his sister in red and gold; Duart's tunic dyed red embroidered with gold and a flowing plaid with yellow stripes; and finally Stewart displaying many colours woven into his plaid like a rainbow! All were displaying their importance, telling us of the Gaelic tradition of emphasizing bright rather than muted colours'.

Crewel Embroidery: The word crewel originally referred to the type of 2-ply wool used in embroidery making chain, tent and stem stitches as we have. Crewel work in Florentine designs (geometric) or Jacobean has a long history but in the sixteenth century crewel work was understood as decorative embroidery in wool on the surface of a closely woven fabric, white fustian (linen and cotton twill weave)[11] — the character chosen to support the weight of the work and for its durability. A pre-eminent example of crewel work is the Bayeux tapestry which inspired our own panels.

'Jacobean' embroidery in the seventeenth century describes the floral design style or the depiction of animals in rolling landscapes, or vines which we often see worked in wool on chairs, fire screens and bed curtains in many of Scotland's castles, stately homes and museums. In the Elizabethan era it appeared much on clothing. Crewel workers were heavily employed in the middle ages to stitch huge wall hangings to help keep rooms warm, sumptuous bed hangings for privacy and to exclude draughts, and for embellishing numerous everyday objects. [Image opposite right of work being sewn for Culross Palace 2010]

Prior to the Union in 1707 Scots exported and imported with the Baltic and across the continent especially France and the Netherlands, so traditional local designs were influenced by the textiles and designs brought back by merchants and travellers. Textiles made for the European market in China and India, particularly Indian wall hangings called palampores, became popular. However there were distinguished local Scottish artists – Lord Cullen's daughter commissioned work dated 1750 from an Aberdeenshire artist[11] – and designs and embroidery materials were being ordered from London at that time.

With further improvements in trade, and the availability of silk threads, 2ply wool crewel work became less popular. When the wealthy required embroidered suits or wedding dresses they were worked professionally and made up by tailors or bought abroad. Professional embroiderers were men who became members of guilds after a seven year apprenticeship. Across the centuries they embroidered ecclesiastical furnishings, vestments and court regalia, but after the Reformation the demand for ecclesiastic embroidery was greatly reduced and they moved their emphasis to secular domestic items. Generally domestic furnishings continued to be designed and embroidered by amateurs and it was imperative for ladies of noble birth to add this to their accomplishments. Many were taught by their governesses or by nuns from abroad, while servant girls did the plain sewing.

Crewel work employs various stitches in wool giving a slightly raised effect, and there is an element of freedom for the embroiderer in the choice of stitch within an outlined shape. We ensured our stitchers had this choice for their panels too. Embroidery techniques have evolved over the centuries and, apart from ecclesiastical embroidery, no fixed conventions are adhered to among contemporary mixed media textile makers.

Crewel work sewn by a group for bed covers for Culross

Our Prestonpans Tapestry panels are a free style of embroidery worked in wool with an element of restrictions on a lovely fine linen with no obvious grid. The linen we used was from Brodie and Middleton, called Ecru, a Scottish linen with a very close weave, the linen's colour complementing the dyes of the Appleton's wools we selected.

An embroidery frame or hoop was required to hold the linen at an even tension while working as this helps the end result. Some used fixed rectangular embroidery frames but the obvious problem here is continually unlacing the attached linen and re-attaching to move along the linen as you sewed. Mostly people used a variety of sizes of hooped frames which they moved around areas within the panels. Some however used newer plastic frames where the plastic side bars snap over and hold the linen onto a fixed rectangular frame.

Most embroiderers were familiar with the Quaker tapestry in Kendal which is slightly shorter than ours with 77 panels depicting the history of Quakers and the D Day Overlord Tapestry at Portsmouth, but there are many other examples of similar community projects created particularly for the Millennium across the UK. We were especially fascinated by the Fishguard Tapestry telling of The Last Invasion of Britain by the French in Pembrokeshire in 1797; Leeds Tapestry, the History of Gotham and the Ipswich Charter Hangings. We have also shared processes with Newfoundland's French Shore Tapestry which is still being worked as well as exploring the story behind The Apocalypse at Angers in France – for many centuries the longest tapestry in the world at 140 metres until nearly 40 metres were lost.

Unlike many artists, Andrew Crummy was deliberately generous in allowing the stitchers to adapt his designs, after consultation, whether to re-design elements or use particular colours they preferred. His 21st century designs are strong images, heavily researched, depicting men preparing for or in battle in 1745 yet envisioned 255 years after the event and conditioned by myth. As with the Bayeux, the Prestonpans Tapestry is

Left detail stitching of a redcoat jacket, and a cannon

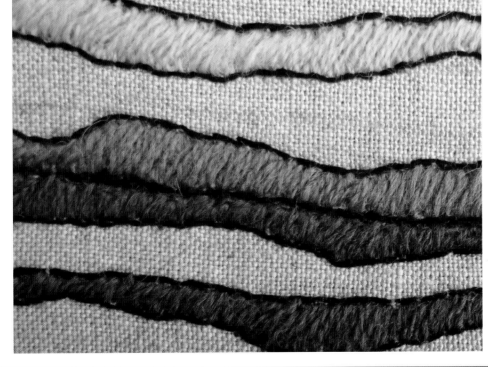

Trees couched, angled straight stitch used for waves, hills and smoke, and a fine example of a house from the Dunblane panel

intended to be hung in public. Like the Bayeux designed at Canterbury in 11th century England, the Prestonpans Tapestry tells its story as a mediaeval strip cartoon. But for the Prestonpans Tapestry Andrew Crummy begged to differ from Bayeux by deliberately giving a perspective on contemporary Scottish life. Bayeux's main purpose had of course been religious to show 'the fulfilment of God's judgement on the violated oath sworn by Harold at Bayeux'.[10]

On individuality: Originally Andrew Crummy wanted everyone to interpret their panels as they wished to allow the individual's character to come through in their stitchery. However the need quickly emerged for considered 'continuity' e.g. in the colour of Bonnie Prince Charlie's attire in connected panels. Nevertheless the Prince was gifted so many different items of clothing at different stages of his campaign that such engineered continuity might well contradict the reality. Despite such 'rules' I do consider that each panel displays the stitcher's individuality Andrew Crummy was so keen to encourage. In common with the Bayeux we began by limiting the number of stitches to be used i.e. Stem stitch for outlining in black to bind the colours together, split, back and laid, couching or filling stitch for rather more. This was because Andrew Crummy designed initially as an artist not an embroiderer, creating rather large areas to be infilled requiring more stitches and we had the timescale we were

following. Along came satin, long and short, seeding, fly, herringbone, French knots, buttonhole, Quaker, chain stitch and maybe one or two made-up for the occasion.

We tried to encourage everyone to sew the outlines first starting with the parallel lines on three sides, and then the shapes within. Firstly to 'catch' the lines before they rubbed off, and secondly, we all got used to the character of the wool and created a rhythm to our sewing. The wool varied slightly in quality, so some used a wax block to run the wool through but another suggestion was to run the wool across the lead of a soft pencil, so that the fibres smoothed out. Stitches 'evolved' for various reasons, and

Lovely legs and socks!

the plaids and tartans brought out the ingenuity in our ladies, inspiring each other's own interpretation.

Who knew how to stitch smoke, grass, strawberries or bog land?

Stranded cotton was used for the fire in the Edinburgh oven for smoothness and colour intensity, and we introduced black cotton for the finer details such as rigging, small objects and figures. Then the idea of gold and silver thread for buttons and rings happened. Suddenly we had to be careful this didn't get out of hand to keep a certain uniformity and not detract from the flow of the story telling. It is hard when a stitcher has a whole directory of stitches and ideas, plus ability, to reign in and keep to a limited 'vocabulary' but still allow each individual to shine. It was very exciting when someone brought their panel and unrolled it for discussion, to see each stage of their beautiful work growing, such a privilege. We all needless to say unpicked areas we were not happy with or decided a better method of stitching.

Once we received the completed panels, often prized from stitchers hands, we had to block them. This means we were stretching the embroidered piece in all directions, evenly, to re-align the fibres of both the linen and wool. Mary Richardson's husband Dave came up with the idea of making boards with carpet gripper nailed on in a slightly larger area than a panel. The panel was then stretched onto the grips checking the embroidered inner measurement was accurate. In some cases this required a good tug! The other method was to pin them out onto clean carpet, with a layer of paper between. Finally we soaked them with a spray bottle of water, which was quite scary until we became used to the groans and twisting pins as the linen shrunk and dried! Every panel benefitted from blocking. Finally we trimmed the panels to a set size before they were machined together and backed with calico. We had a great team of ladies preparing each step required.

I mentioned wigs earlier, and what fun was had sewing them! Depending on the scale of the head, bullion knots, split stitch, French knots in varying thickness of threads, were all worked so effectively.

233

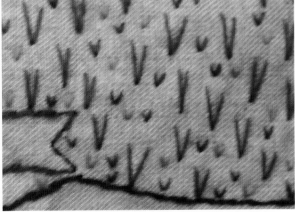

How to sew bog land and strawberries!

This stunning Prestonpans Tapestry was embroidered in record time, just 15 months, with the greatest loving care and commitment to tell the story of the Battle of Prestonpans. All who designed and stitched it sincerely hope that over the coming centuries thousands even millions will enjoy and learn from it as much as we have in its creation.

References

1. J. Telfer Dunbar, *The History of Highland Dress*, (1962).
   (1a) p89 *Bonnie Prince Charlie*, Henrietta Tayler, London 1845
   (1b) Reproduced from the *Scottish Historical Review*, 1908

2. Hugh Cheape, *Tartan – The Highland Habit*, 1991

3. Captain Burt, *Letters from a Gentleman in the North of Scotland* (1730). He was a civil engineer surveying roads for General Wade 1720s

4. James Logan, *The Scottish Gael*, vol. 1 (1831)

5. J Ray, *Complete History of Rebellion*, (1749).

6. www.macfarlanescompany.org

7. Act of Proscription: "That from and after the First Day of August 1747, no man or boy within that part of Great Britain called Scotland, other than such as shall be employed as Officers and Soldiers of His Majesty's Forces, shall on any pretext whatsoever, wear or put on the clothes, commonly called Highland clothes (that is to say) the Plaid, Philabeg, or little kilt, Trowes, Shoulder-Belts, or any part whatever of what peculiarly belongs to the Highland Garb; and that no tartan or party-coloured plaid or stuff shall be used for Great coats or upper coats, and if any such person shall presume after the first said day of August, to wear or put on the aforesaid garments or any part of them, every person so offending.... shall be liable to be transported to any of His Majesty's plantations beyond the seas, there to remain for the space of seven years."
   The exception was made in the Act for those serving in the army where the Highland regiments wore the 'Government pattern '.

8. Anita Quye and High Cheape, *Costume, vol*.42, (2008).

9. James Philip of Almerieclose, *Grameid* (1691)

10. B. Snook, *English Embroidery*: Bell & Hyman; 1974.

11. Margaret Swain, *Scottish Embroidery Medieval to Modern*, Batsford 1986.

Further reading

Avril Hart and Susan North, *Historical Fashion in Detail*, V&A Publications; 2002.

Hugh Cheape, *Tartan The Highland Habit*, National Museums Scotland; 1991.

J. Telfer Dunbar, *History of Highland Dress*, Universtiy Press Glasgow; 1962.

Jan Messant, *The Bayeux Tapestry Embroiderers' Story*, Redwood Books Ltd.; 1999.

The Times Newspaper, June 17th, 1995: Hugh Cheape, the museum's curator, was asked in 1987 to authenticate a piece of tartan from the archives of Stonyhurst College in Lancashire (northwest England). We know about a kilt given to Prince Charles researched by Mr Hugh Cheape, one of the previous curators at the National Museum of Scotland, which resulted in the tracing and reconstruction of the tartan worn by Bonnie Prince Charlie after his flight from Culloden. The blue-green tartan, with red, black and yellow stripes is different from any of those known today, which were introduced in the 19th Century. There was a piece of paper with the cloth stating that it was part of a kilt left by Bonnie Prince Charlie on the Island of Glass on April 30th. 1746. This was identified as the Hebridean island of Scalpay, known as Eilean Glas in Gaelic, and it was discovered that the Prince had sheltered there with a taxman called Campbell.

There was also documentary evidence that the Prince had been given a "sute of cloaths" at the home of the MacDonalds of Kingsburgh by Catriona MacDonald (a MacGregor) who welcomed him there. Several days after he left government troops destroyed the house. Campbell, the taxman, was reported to the English by the minister on Scalpay, but when they arrived they were unable to land. The scrap of tartan is believed to be from the kilt given to the Prince by Catriona MacDonald and left at the house of Campbell. It was analyzed by Dr. Anita Quye of the museum's conservation unit who identified the dyes in the tartan using liquid chromatography and spectroscopy – all the dyes are natural ones used in the 18th Century.

Here's to new friends!!

18th Century Architecture Revisited

by Gareth Bryn-Jones

The landscape through which both Jacobite and Government armies marched in 1745 has in many places, and particularly in the western Highlands and islands, changed little in the intervening centuries. Other areas have undergone radical change as agriculture, industry, forestry and urban growth have made their mark.

Some of the buildings, structures and towns documented as having played a part in the '45, such as Preston Tower, are largely unchanged. Many more have however been altered, improved or either wholly or partially demolished. Some buildings depicted on the tapestry, most notably Dunblane Cathedral, have actually been rebuilt to reflect their earlier forms.

In the north and west of the country the buildings of the mid-18th Century were largely of vernacular origin. Small, long and low dwellings built entirely using locally sourced materials predominated while the largest buildings were usually those remaining from earlier times, specifically the fortified stone tower houses and castles of the wealthier landowners. That is not to say that the Highlands were devoid of contemporary architecture and some substantial interpretations of neo-classical buildings were built. Some of the earlier fortified buildings were also enlarged and altered to give them a more domestic appearance. Other more middling houses also started to appear, less defensive in their design and owing more to the symmetrical and classically proportioned houses found in the lowlands.

As the clans moved south and east they would have been aware of significant changes in the buildings they encountered, largely reflecting the relative wealth of the regions they were passing through. Around the towns and cities Scotland had already undergone significant agricultural improvements and the simple vernacular farm dwellings were being replaced with larger and more formally designed building groups, their

design following patterns developed to improve agricultural production. New buildings were almost always built from locally quarried stone (either from the ground or *robbed* from earlier buildings) with glazed timber sash windows. Slated or tiled roofs predominated in new works but many thatched buildings remained, although in Edinburgh the use of thatch had been outlawed by Act of Parliament as early as 1624.

Within the cities and towns many buildings from the 16th and 17th centuries remained in use, often rising high and perhaps incorporating timber jetties or galleries. The density of building may have been oppressive or astounding to Highland visitors more accustomed to open spaces and low buildings. Many of Scotland's Burghs, including Edinburgh and Stirling, were still constrained in part at least by their medieval boundaries and walls.

Industrialisation had also taken hold, particularly on the banks of the Firth of Forth where coal was being exported as well as being used to fire the growing local industries. These included salt panning, brewing, pottery making and chemical and (whale) oil production and processing. Prestonpans itself was a developing centre of industry, positioned between the rich agricultural lands to the east, the Firth of Forth to the north and Edinburgh ten miles, barely a day's march, to the west. The town was however still divided, with the Burgh of Preston occupying the higher ground above the industry, which was strung out along the coast.

When Andrew Crummy asked for advice in recreating the buildings featured on the tapestry it seemed like a straightforward enough request. It quickly dawned on us however, during our trip to Borrodale and the west coast that, while many of the buildings which had played a significant part in the story survived, they had invariably been altered, modernised or extended. In many instances few, if any, illustrations of the buildings as they would have appeared in 1745 seemed to have survived.

We have not taken an entirely academic approach to the recreation of the buildings. Some were straightforward and well recorded and have hopefully been depicted with a good degree of accuracy. Some buildings were obscure, poorly recorded and much altered. With these we have taken a few liberties, informed by what scarce contemporary illustrations do exist and by reference to surviving buildings of comparable type. Finally, some locations proved too obscure to determine their appearance with any degree of accuracy at all. There may of course be surviving records of these locations but we were unable to trace them as stitching proceeded. These locations have either been reduced on the finished tapestry or in two instances they have disappeared altogether!

The following examples are intended to illustrate the approach that has been taken throughout. Details of other buildings are held by the Trust and any further enquiries will be attended to as best we are able.

1. Borrodale House

The Battle Trust quite deliberately spent several days staying at Borrodale in October 2009 to be in the place where the Prince had awaited the response of the Clan Chiefs to his call for support. The house itself has been much altered since 1745 and is probably substantially larger now than it was then. It is clear that the current building does however incorporate substantial elements from the time of the '45. The earliest portion of the house would appear to be the low building on the right of the illustration. This seems to have been retained as an outhouse, as has the fascinating creel house, which projects from the more substantial two-storey house probably erected in the early 1700s. How this curious arrangement came about is unclear but it is likely that these three connected buildings form the core of the property in which the Prince lodged. The photograph of the house as it is today tells the story of the intervening years in which the house has been extended to the west, the windows enlarged and, in 1864, substantially remodelled and further enlarged to designs prepared by Architect Philip Webb. A farm group, which includes a huge and decidedly un-Scottish split barn, was also added by Webb and this work remains as his only surviving substantial Scottish commission.

Above top: Extract showing Borrodale from General Roy's survey map, c1750

Above left: Sketch showing Borrodale House as it may have been in 1745 and a similar sketch showing nearby Dalilea without its 20th century embelishments

Above right: Borrodale House in 2009, showing extensions and alterations by Philip Webb

Despite its colourful history there seem to be few surviving illustrations of the Castle prior to its destruction in 1746. The clearest image of the Castle dates from after its ruination and the tapestry image is based loosely on this sketch. The building is a fine Tower House, with a basic L shaped plan and a distinctive roofline, punctuated with steep gables and turreted bartisans and towers. The remains of some of these embellishments now lie amongst the rubble strewn around the foot of the castle. Parts of the castle rose a full six floors but visitors today will find a fenced and dangerous ruin, which has continued to deteriorate despite bold attempts at consolidation.

3. Inveresk and Old St. Michael's Church

Panel 62 shows Inveresk, just five miles to the west of Prestonpans. Inveresk was, until the late 1600s, a relatively small and unremarkable village. It was however to change in character as a number of substantial mansion houses were constructed over the following century. Several of these houses are depicted in the panel and can still be seen, their external appearance having changed little.

The panel also shows St Michael's Church, one building which the visitor to Inveresk today will not see. The church was demolished to allow for the construction of the existing building, which opened in 1805, but has been recorded in a number of sketches and written accounts. Some of these accounts and drawings relate to the Battle of Pinkie, which was fought in the fields to the south and east of the church in 1547. None can be regarded as precise representations of the church and so the sketch for the tapestry panel is based on an interpretation of the several sketches and written descriptions as well as comparison with surviving (if extensively altered) medieval churches in the area, such as Whitecross, Seton and

2. Invergarry Castle

Tapestry **panel 30** depicts Loch Oich with Invergarry Castle resting above on its promontory, Creagan an Fhithich, the Rock of the Raven. The castle had ancient origins but had been rebuilt on at least two occasions before it was extensively remodelled in the early 17th century. The castle was however damaged by fire in 1654, just prior to its further bespoiling by soldiers under General Monk's command. In 1727 the castle was again rebuilt, this time by new owner Thomas Rawlinson, although soon after it returned to Glengarry hands. In 1746 the castle was again destroyed, this time with gunpowder by the Hanoverian army, and it was never rebuilt.

Left: Engraving showing Invergarry Castle in the late 18th Century, following its final abandonment

Contemporary drawing showing Inveresk Old St. Michael's Church during the Battle of Pinkie, 1547

Aberlady. The church was clearly of medieval origin but may have evolved over many years and we have tried to show this in the panel. Old St. Michael's final minister, Dr Alexander Carlyle, was also its most famous and Dr Carlyle described the old building's unusual features such as its two rows of aisles and double galleries. One of its most curious features was the double tower, which comprised a substantial round tower immediately adjacent to a more conventional square tower. Perhaps the circular tower was simply a large stair tower but perhaps it was a remnant of a much earlier building? Later illustrations of the church are also unclear and some show a spire, which was added to the square tower towards the end of its life.

4. Dunblane Cathedral

Very little interpretation or conjecture was required for the image of Dunblane Cathedral, shown in **panel 39**. There are several engravings, drawings and paintings of the building dating from the 1700s and earlier, including two views dating from the late 17th century from John Slezer's *Theatrum Scotiae*. The building shown in these is however quite different from the one seen today. By 1745 only the choir and the earlier tower of the Cathedral remained in use, while the nave and west front were roofless, derelict and decaying. Sections of the masonry were collapsing and to the north there was evidence that the building was being used as a quarry, providing stone for use in constructing new buildings. Dunblane was a developing industrial town centred on its mills, which were powered by the Allan Water, and there was a need to house an influx of workers. It is perhaps more surprising that so little of the building was actually removed during this time and in the closing years of the 19th century major repairs to the building were carried out under the direction of Architect Rowand Anderson. These continued over several years and work on the interior was completed in 1914, this time to designs prepared by Robert Lorimer.

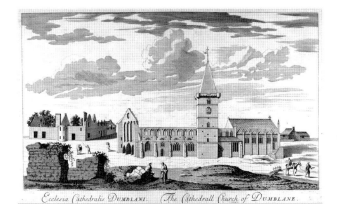

Ecclesia Cathedralis DUMBLANI. The Cathedrall Church of DUMBLANE.

Below Left: Engraving showing Dunblane Cathedral from the south west, 1821

Left: Engraving showing Dunblane Cathedral from the south around 1693, from Slezer's Theatrum Scotiae

Below right: Dunblane Cathedral from the south east, as rebuilt.

DUNBLANE CATHEDRAL.

239

5. Preston House and Tower

Preston House and more specifically its substantial and extensive stone garden walls played a critical part in the Battle. Many retreating Hanoverian government troops found themselves unable to climb or to avoid the walls and were cut down by the advancing Jacobite army. The role the wall had played in events was well recognised and respected in the aftermath of the battle and the government army ensured that the walls around Culloden were more comprehensively pierced in advance of that battle.

Preston House itself was surrounded by extensive and well-documented gardens. These are depicted in several of the contemporary battle maps. Less is known of the house itself however. It was probably built in the early 18th Century to replace Preston Tower, which had been severely damaged by fire. The tower is also depicted in the panel, ruinous as it appeared then and does now, with its curious roofline resulting from its extension upwards in the 17th Century. The design of Preston House

mirrored several other Scottish houses of the period and comprised a central block with pavilions clasped by curving wings. The lamentably derelict Mavisbank House near Loanhead, designed in the 1720s by William Adam, is perhaps a close match in character, if not detail, to Preston House.

By the late 19th century Preston House was in a derelict state and when the Royal Commission on the Ancient and Historical Monuments of Scotland visited to record the remains of the house in 1924 there was little remaining above the ground floor walls. There are now no standing remains of the house itself, although sections of the garden walls do survive. The panel depicts the house as it may have appeared in 1745 and is based primarily on depictions of the property on contemporary maps, drawn to illustrate the Battle, and the 1924 RCAHMS survey drawings.

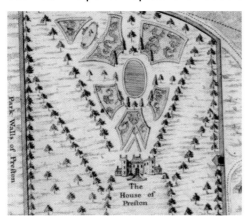

Above: Photograph showing Preston Tower, which has survived its replacement, Preston House

Preston House 1745: Extract from a Battle plan drawn in 1745 showing Preston House and its gardens and walls

6. Callendar House

This imposing house has a long and complex history. Its origins may relate to the Roman occupation of Scotland and some of the most impressive sections of the Antonine Wall pass to the immediate north of the house. Close by are the remains of a 10th century timber hall. The house is a development of a 14th or 15th Century stone tower house and by the early 18th Century it had grown, incrementally, into a substantial dwelling. The house, as it is depicted in **panel 43**, had grown into a formal and basically symmetrical classical building, very much in the fashion of the time. This is not the appearance of the house today however, for it was again extensively remodelled in the mid-19th century gaining a profusion of French medieval turrets, steeply pitched roofs and eventually large projecting bay windows. Callendar House has been repaired by Falkirk Council and now houses an impressive museum, which includes the working early 19th century kitchen. The external wall of the building depicted in the panel can still be seen in the entrance hall of the current house.

The panel also depicts the tower of St.Michael's church in Linlithgow, which is immediately adjacent to Linlithgow Palace. The tower was, in 1745, topped with its fine stone crown but this was removed in response to concerns about its stability in 1821. The current aluminium spire was constructed in 1964.

7. Ruthven Barracks

There had been a fort on the raised mound at Ruthven since at least the 13th century and a more suitable site for controlling the passage to and from the north would be hard to imagine. The mound rises from the glacial valley as if man-made, although its origins are probably also as a glacial drumlin. The earlier castles were however cleared away in the aftermath of the 1715 Rebellion and the Barracks were largely completed in 1721. They formed a vital part of the Government's strategy to control the Highlands and followed designs based largely on functional principles. The barracks were capable of housing over 100 troops and were extended in the 1730s to incorporate stables for use by the dragoons. The stables can be seen to the side of the main barrack blocks and enclosure. When the Jabobite army reached Ruthven [Panel 34] it found it defended by just 12 soldiers but they successfully held out and the building survived.

The Barracks were less fortunate however in February of the following year, when the Jacobite army returned, this time with artillery, and the

Right: Drawing showing Callendar House as extended in the later 1700s

Left: Sketch showing the possible appearance of Callendar House in 1745

Right: Photograph showing Callendar House as extended and embellished in the 19th Century

242

A GARRISON OF S...

small garrison surrendered. The building remained largely intact however, until it was sacked and burned by the remains of the Jacobite army on 17th April 1746. It was never rebuilt.

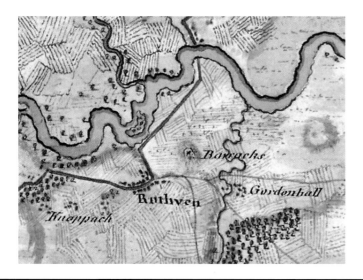

Extract from General Roy's military survey of Scotland, showing Ruthven Barracks in context

8. Edinburgh – baking the bread

Some things never change and so it might seem with Edinburgh, instantly recognisable from **panel 19**. Edinburgh has in fact changed very substantially since it became embroiled in the 1745 rebellion. The soaring and tightly packed buildings depicted in the panel (only slightly heightened for artistic effect) made Edinburgh one of the most densely populated cities anywhere. The city was however already becoming the centre for the Scottish Enlightenment (David Hume was born in 1711 in one of the tenements on Lawnmarket) despite having such cramped and apparently insanitary conditions. Substantial tenements fronted the street while smaller and often poorly built buildings spread to the rear, filling much of the rig ground. The bakehouses, breweries, workshops and booths were packed within the tightly confined boundaries of the city, still constrained by its hilltop geography and defensive walls. Few of these buildings survive today however.

In the years following 1745 the city boundaries were extended, the Nor' Loch drained and, in 1765-66 a competition was held for designs for a New Town, to be built to the north of the city. Access to the new development was formed by breaking through the city's original northern boundaries and this was followed, in the 19th Century, by a series of city Improvement Acts. One such Act, in 1867, had been prompted by the collapse of one of the substantial buildings to the north side of the High Street. The improvements invariably involved the demolition of many of the earlier tenements and often the formation of new streets, running at right angles to the High Street and connecting it with the New Town and further developments to the south. If any part of the image of Edinburgh stands out then it is surely the stone Crown on the tower of the church of St. Giles'. The crown survives, unlike the similar crown of the tower of St. Michael's in Linlithgow, although the church itself, hidden from view behind the tenements, was extensively remodelled and cleared of much of its later medieval alterations in the 19th Century.

Left: View of the High Street, Edinburgh in the 18th Century

Right: View of Edinburgh from the north, from Slezer's Theatrum Scotiae, c1695

9. The Netherbow Port, Edinburgh

Edinburgh was not well defended when the Jacobite army arrived in September 1745 but it was not completely without protection and was still largely confined within its walls and gates. Netherbow Port stood at the east end of the High Street, near to where the well-known World's End bar now stands. It was a substantial stone built gate-house with turreted towers facing east to either side of the single gateway and a clock tower rising centrally above. The inner face of the building, as shown in **panel 52**, was simpler. There had been a gate in the Netherbow since the 12th Century but the stone building, which confronted the Jacobite army, probably dated from the 16th Century and was similar in character to the foreworks at Stirling Castle and to other near-contemporary royal works at Holyrood and Falkland. The gateway was not however maintained in good condition and it was demolished in 1764. That was not the end of the story though and it was reconstructed on Edinburgh's Meadows as part of the 1886 International Exhibition of Science and Art. The Netherbow Port

Above: Engraving showing the east front of the Netherbow Port – as captured in the tapestry panel

Left: Engraving showing the west front of the Netherbow Port

Right: Sketch showing the Netherbow Port being dismantled in 1764

was demolished for a second time shortly after when attempts to have it retained as a lasting monument to the exhibition failed.

*

To conclude therefore, we trust it will be appreciated that we took such steps as were reasonably possible to accurately represent the buildings along the Prince's and Sir John Cope's routes in 1745. We also trust that the reader or viewer will accept that some artistic licence has been taken and will excuse the [hopefully occasional] indiscretion.

Conserving and Learning our Nation's History through The Prestonpans Tapestry

by Fiona Campbell

The Message

The Jacobite Rebellion of 1745 is deeply embedded in the heritage of the British nation, and an important chapter in its history. It reads as a captivating tale of dynastic nationalism, clan loyalty and rivalry, momentous victories and colossal defeats. It is set against the backdrop of tradition and modernisations, cultural change, and social restructuring. It is also a story of human endeavour, from the lowliest clansman or red-coated soldier, to the lofty ambitions and gritty will of Charles Edward Stuart. The Prince, fondly remembered by the world as *Bonnie Prince Charlie*, set sail from France to Scotland in order to defend his own family heritage, to offer an alternative to the world as it was. For too long, the telling of the '45 has been dominated by the tragedy of Culloden, and the sense of loss engendered by the failure of the Rising, the destruction of the clan system, and the subsequent persecution and depopulation of the Highlands and their culture. Although significant, the tendency to dwell on defeat, to read the story as some sad inevitable tragedy, can overshadow some of the more motivational, enduring, and exciting messages of the '45.

The time has come, then, to remember the other side of the campaigns: the human stories, the local stories, and the important message of Victory, Hope, and Ambition. This is the message of the Battle of Prestonpans, of Charles Edward's efforts and his successes, and it is as important as his ultimate failure. It is also the unofficial motto of the Battle of Prestonpans (1745) Heritage Trust, and of The Prestonpans Tapestry. Regardless of whether your viewpoint might be Jacobite or Hanoverian, this is a message which can captivate and inspire, and which needs to be shared.

The Prestonpans Tapestry is Scotland's latest endeavour to provide detailed and accessible interpretation of the events which led to Bonnie Prince Charlie's triumphant victory on September 21st 1745. This pivotal moment in the Prince's campaign represents the success of a young (only twenty-five years old at the time of the battle), courageous man, filled with ambition and supported by loyal clansmen. Significantly, the Tapestry ends soon after the battle, and does not continue to the end of the Rising. Its lasting message is one of hope.

The Prestonpans Tapestry is a project which combines local stories and traditions regarding the '45, and the talents of diverse individuals, and creates from them a single entity to tell a continuous story. In this regard, it has always been about bringing the story of the Battle of Prestonpans out into the wider national community. The next step is to ensure that the stories and experiences which have been concentrated in it are now spread to as broad an audience as possible. Crucial to this mission, and the Tapestry's role as a nationally important project, is its relevance and effectiveness in an educational context.

The Precedents

This Tapestry is, of course, not the first of its type. Rather, it builds upon a well-established artistic heritage and, more recently, a proven track-record of successful appeal. For centuries tapestries have been created as artistic decorations, and to promote moral and political messages. They were praised for their ability to be easily transported, and to capture beauty, intricate detail, and vivid colour. The design and techniques used to create such works of art changed depending upon where and when they were created. The Bayeux Tapestry for instance, is not a classically woven tapestry but rather a piece of embroidery. That it is known as a tapestry creates the artistic precedent which Prestonpans is following.

In the present day, the thought of a tapestry transports our minds back into the medieval, renaissance, or arts and crafts periods. Tapestries were usually the preserve of the wealthy, of kings and aristocrats, often portraying mottos and emblems, and crucially able to be transported when royalty relocated around their numerous households and castles. These are also themes relevant to The Prestonpans Tapestry, dealing with themes of dynastic struggle, and designed for ease of transportation in anticipation of touring exhibitions. In addition to the aesthetic appeal of tapestries, it must also be remembered that they also held a more practical function; tapestries provided insulation and often helped to ensure privacy within the household. These are perhaps less relevant to the modern tapestry.

In the twentieth century, tapestries are first and foremost intended to display a narrative history, and to preserve a tradition or story. They not only preserve the art of their physical creation, but also have a role as educational resources to inform and engage the public. In this, they have a proven track record. Take for instance *The Last Invasion* tapestry, created by the Fishguard Arts Society, which depicts a failed French landing in Wales in 1797. Once a little known event, great credit is now given to the tapestry for helping to ensure that the event is now an internationally recognised episode. The Quaker Tapestry, housed in Kendal, and the respected Overlord Embroidery in Portsmouth are both also highly regarded. The message of the latter was of such significance that the original watercolours are now housed within the Pentagon in the United States of America. The Prestonpans Tapestry, once launched in the summer of 2010 has every chance of following in these footsteps. The Tapestry has the potential, being as portable as tapestries were always intended, to cross national and cultural boundaries as well as to appeal beyond them.

Heritage tapestries have therefore demonstrated the potential appeal of tapestries as artworks. British school children not only cross the Channel to visit Bayeux, but there is also a substantial appetite for the faithful nineteenth century copy of it in Reading (and there are further copies too, across the globe). Major tapestries like Bayeux, Reading, and Overlord have all proven their worth and popularity, gaining widespread recognition, and also each preparing appropriate educational programmes to support them. All have provided lessons and inspiration for the Prestonpans project.

Relevance and Appeal

This new Tapestry can assist in the preservation of a significant moment in the nation's history, whilst connecting individuals together by identifying their national heritage. In order to join the time-tested Bayeux Tapestry, or the more recent but equally remarkable Overlord Embroidery (commissioned in 1968) on the pedestal of internationally recognised projects, The Prestonpans Tapestry must prove itself to be an effective means of engaging audiences of all ages in its subject matter. The means of achieving this have been built into the project from its inception.

Similarly to other such artworks, The Prestonpans Tapestry follows events in a narrative sequence, in this case beginning with Charles Edward Stuart's departure from Rome to his victory at the Battle of Prestonpans in 1745. Unlike Bayeux, the image is not continuous but presented as a series of individual panels, or scenes, in a variety of dimensions and perspectives but all in a unified style and colour scheme. This preserves the integrity of the whole body, whilst allowing the visitor to segregate events into neat parcels, making the Tapestry easy to navigate. It also allows the Tapestry to scene-change, from one army to another, importantly allowing a balanced portrayal of events within both armies as they marched towards a shared climax. Viewing and exploring the Tapestry is therefore easy to enjoy, and the chronological sequence (helped by the thorough labelling of people, dates, and places) creates a helpful environment for learning. Effectively, The Prestonpans Tapestry represents a giant comic-strip of the '45, a comparison which should not be overlooked when it is presented to the younger generation.

Of course, if people are to learn from the Tapestry then they cannot simply be enjoying a comic: they must be receiving an accurate interpretation of events. The historical authenticity of the scenes which have been captured within the elegant stitches of this embroidery has been overseen by the Battle Trust, supported by Martin Margulies and Arran Johnston, both of whom are published writers on the '45. The intended result is an accurate depiction of Bonnie Prince Charlie's epic journey, the people and cultures involved, and the landscape in which it all took place. In addition to depicting the key moments of the campaign – the raising of the Prince's standard by the Duke of Atholl, the fall of Edinburgh, or indeed the Battle of Prestonpans itself – Creative Director Andrew Crummy has successfully designed the Tapestry to contain images of daily life in the eighteenth century: the clothing of different social ranks, the transportation and weaponry available, the architecture of castles, towns and villages, and the changeable terrain and climate of Scotland. All these can be sought, identified, and recognised in The Prestonpans Tapestry. Some things are

Education and The Prestonpans Tapestry: A Summary

An Educational Resource:

- Depicting one of Scotland's most significant battles of the eighteenth century, and preserving the stories which surround it.
- Represents the importance of 1745 in the development and perception of a Scottish identity.
- By ending with the Prince's victory, the Tapestry offers a message of hope and ambition, encouraging personal endeavour.
- Showing scenes of eighteenth century Scotland's material culture, architecture and landscape, the Tapestry is a vibrant visual aid to Scottish heritage studies.
- The Tapestry supports the National Curriculum of Excellence through its use of supporting resources (worksheets, crafts, object handling) in order to develop personal skills, independent problem solving, investigation and discovery.
- It is truly cross-curricular in what can be gained from a supported study of the Tapestry.

A National Stimulus:

- The Battle of Prestonpans was a stimulus for creative activity. The Tapestry can do the same.
- The scenes of the Tapestry can work as a spring-board for a celebration and study of Scottish song and folklore, as well as art, craft and design.
- Supporting activities born from the Tapestry can increase the understanding of Scots language, the role of music in motivation and identity creation, and the works of national figures such as Burns and Scott.
- The Tapestry provides a context for other existing resources, including the BattleGame which provides an entertaining, competitive and informative way of understanding the process of the Battle, whilst building numeracy skills. Living History classroom visits help bring the Tapestry to life, and permit children to interact with the history.
- The Prestonpans Tapestry is national in its coverage, in its creation, and in its appeal. It has the potential to become internationally significant and generate fresh waves of interest.

familiar, some things have changed. All these details combine to enhance the Tapestry, becoming not just a national community art project, but an educational resource for the '45 and eighteenth century Scotland. The Prestonpans Tapestry thus has a role in developing our understanding of the nation's heritage, with a value easily discernible in a self-aware nation such as modern Scotland.

The 1745 Rising is not only important to British heritage, but it also has a well-established appeal. Certainly visitors to Scotland are frequently exposed to the '45, either by the images of the Bonnie Prince on their shortbread tins or the wide selection of Jacobite museum collections scattered across the county. The narrative of the event, however, crosses national boundaries: plaques and monuments can be found in Kendal, Derby, and even London. The Prestonpans Tapestry takes us further still, with scenes in France and Italy also. The appeal of the '45 has also

followed Scots emigrant culture across the world, and finds bases in Canada, America, Australasia, and beyond. Accordingly, as an asset of cultural significance the Prestonpans Tapestry appeals to international audiences by exemplifying awareness of Scotland and the Scots, particularly in the wake of the *Year of the Homecoming*. By capturing a narrative of the people and conditions of the nation in the period, The Prestonpans Tapestry can provide an insight into the lives of these people and characterise the political climate which provided the catalyst for dramatic social change. Certainly, since the Tapestry is designed in order to be transportable, it has the potential to unite nations with a common heritage by exploring their shared association with the '45.

The Prestonpans Tapestry, then, has an extremely broad appeal simply in terms of the significance of the subject matter it portrays. On top of this, it is an exceptional example of a broad-based collaborative community initiative across the nation. Each panel has been created by highly skilled and dedicated volunteers from diverse communities, which together chart the route of Charles Edward Stuart and his opponents. Celebrating the work of these communities and individuals across Scotland, traditional needlework techniques have been put to excellent use in creating an artwork of national importance. As a result, each of the one hundred and four panels of the Tapestry reveals its own unique story, and as can be seen from the pages of this book, it is as much a social document for 2010 as 1745. For those interested in life-long learning, the Tapestry has a value which therefore goes beyond a focus on Britain in the eighteenth century, but also embraces aspects of traditional craft, oral history, and contemporary art. All this expands and enhances its value as a resource for knowledge and understanding, for a wide audience of varied age and background.

The Tapestry as an Educational Tool

However, it is perhaps the younger generations who have most to gain from The Prestonpans Tapestry. There is perhaps no better narrative presentation of the first stages of the 1745 Rising, in terms of visual presentation, thoroughness, and accuracy. The style of the artwork and the bright vivid colours mean the Tapestry has the required appeal to engage the primary school audience. They will see a giant comic-strip, not an embroidery. It will also impress with its scale, and the diversity of the images portrayed. However, The Prestonpans Tapestry is not just to be seen as a means of telling a story: it is cross-curricular, and this is crucial in the current educational environment.

In order to lay the foundations for such engagement, and in order for it to achieve its full educational potential, the Prestonpans Tapestry will be supported from its opening tour by a wide range of activity sheets, aimed mainly at primary school audiences. A developing catalogue of educational worksheets will support the Tapestry in order to provide both entertainment and quality of educational services. As the Tapestry travels on tour, a loan box containing replica artefacts and clothing will accompany it. In the earliest stages of the Tapestry's life, the aims are limited, but in the longer term this is the basis for a programme of richly rewarding school visits. The Prestonpans Tapestry has all the potential to become the stimulus for a whole package of educational experiences.

The role of the Tapestry as a stimulus for further learning is vital to its

long-term significance on a national stage. Due to its scale, it is not likely that the Tapestry will be able to visit individual schools, and so it is important that it finds a residence which permits access to school groups. There are numerous activity-sheet based tasks, such as a Tapestry trail, which can be used to engage the children with the Tapestry. Established techniques of museum education programmes can be enacted to encourage individuals to work both within teams and independently, to enhance the confidence of the learners and to promote wider independent learning and social skills.

The nature of the National Curriculum and educational techniques in historical studies are developing constantly, with an increasing emphasis on activities which develop skill sets beyond simply knowledge of a particular subject-matter. Fortunately, the Tapestry has within it a significant amount of potential for developing education programmes based on these expectations. It lends itself to an interactive, creative form of primary education, due to its flexible educational prospective.

The topics included within the Scottish History curriculum are those which are considered important in the development of a sense of national identity, including of course the '45. The Tapestry is relevant to the Scottish curriculum's *The Jacobite* module, for those schools which choose to teach it, and the general requirement of Key Stage 2 History to help, 'build a picture of Scotland's heritage.' It is also able to assist in a more general appreciation of Scottish culture and geography, amongst other things. Therefore, the Tapestry is a useful resource in supporting the National Curriculum of Excellence, which is currently of pivotal importance in the strategy for primary development. This strategy applies not only to the schools themselves, but it also has implications for museums and exhibitions, which are now expected to provide support to the wider campaign for cross-curricular skills development. In order to engage children effectively, and indeed to encourage schools to promote visiting it, The Prestonpans Tapestry needs to fulfil these requirements.

Fortunately, the Tapestry is able to enhance the education process by moving away from book-based learning and encouraging children to learn their history through the artwork of the Tapestry. Nor is it just history which can be learned. Children should be encouraged to follow the progress of the armies through the landscape of Scotland, exploring how the terrain – well researched and accurately presented – affects events and cultures. How does the Tapestry's portrayal of Invergarry Castle, resplendent in its loch-side location, compare to the tumbled ruins visible today? Are the landmarks of eighteenth century Edinburgh recognisable in the modern city? These are the tasks which make the children focus on the smaller details of the Tapestry, and which make it relevant to their own lives. In an ideal world, a visit to the Tapestry would be the stimulus for visits elsewhere, to discover the physical remains of the '45 story. The advantage of the nationwide coverage of the events described is that there should be something relevant within reach of most communities.

The Prestonpans Tapestry is the latest incarnation of the Battle of Prestonpans' established role as a stimulus for literature and art. This is a point which should be developed through the Tapestry's education programme. Art is an obvious subject, emphasising the Tapestry's importance as an artwork as well as a heritage project, and all manner of artistic activities are able to support it. In particular, children will be encouraged to make their own drawings of scenes, or perhaps to show a scene from their own life in the style of the Tapestry. Music and poetry are, however, equally important. Charles Edward Stuart himself was a capable

musician, whilst there is a wide repertoire of songs and poetry which has been inspired by the Battle: here are skills which can be developed and encouraged through the use of the Tapestry. The exploration of famous Scottish tunes such as *Hey Johnny Cope*, and the national anthem, and the works of iconic national figures such as Robert Burns and Walter Scott, can all be facilitated on the back of the Tapestry. Individuals can thus explore the Scots language and the ways history can be transmitted through music and popular literature. This form of learning will capture young imaginations, promoting the importance of oral history as well as the more familiar document-based narrative. A study of Scottish music would highlight how music can be morale-boosting at the time, can portray a certain political message, but could also show how modern national identity has its roots in the past. Again, the relevance of the '45 and the legacy of the Battle of Prestonpans are made obvious and engaging.

The Future

Of course, it is not anticipated that the Prestonpans Tapestry will exist in isolation. Whether visiting as a family or as a school, the learner will need supporting resources like the activity sheets and handling boxes to direct their education experience and channel their engagement. On the next level, a school visit would be supported by follow-up activities along the lines advised by the Tapestry's Teacher's Notes. Further still, there has also been an increasing emphasis of 'living history' presentation as an educational tool in museums and schools, and the Battle of Prestonpans (1745) Heritage Trust has made important progress in developing their own professional programme of visits to local schools. These dramatic appearances further explain the context of the '45, and their use of the purpose-built battle-game table adds to the entertainment and learning experience. When they are eventually combined with the Tapestry itself, these resources come together to create an extremely engaging package. At the moment, the Trust's schools programme performs at the school itself, something unsuited to the Tapestry. When the Tapestry is installed in a longer-term home, however, and the other resources are put in place around it, the educational potential of the Battle of Prestonpans becomes immense.

Although much attention has been given to the Tapestry's value to Primary Schools, it must be considered that there is no age restriction on its value. There is also a significant opportunity for the Tapestry to be re-visited by pupils as part of a Secondary curriculum. It is perhaps then that it might be used as an educational resource through its role as an artwork, relevant to craft and design courses. Teenage audiences are likely to have a more developed historical understanding, and would be less reliant on the narrative form of the Tapestry, but might find an alternative value in it. If the pupil had visited as part of their primary education, a repeat visit at a later date would provide a linking force within a learner's longer term experience, and offer a sense of familiarity for pupils during their transition of schooling.

The Battle of Prestonpans has already witnessed significant forward progress in terms of its interpretation and accessibility. With roots established in supporting events like the annual re-enactments and living history encampments, the production of children's guides to the battle, and the growing popularity of interpretive school visits, the educational value of the Battle can only increase in the coming years. The centre-piece to all future programmes, the fundamental narrative resource which will act as both focus and stimulus, will be the Prestonpans Tapestry.

The Tapestry holds an appeal which is tangible on a local, national, and even international level. Through this, surely one of Scotland's largest community artworks, the legacy of the 1745 campaign may now preserved in a dynamic and timeless manner. Like other embroideries and tapestries of its type, the Prestonpans Tapestry has the potential to develop the understanding of our nation's heritage, and provide a crucial role in its teaching. Used effectively, it can provide a deeper insight into topics within the curriculum, help to build creative skills, confidence, and an ability to identify with the past. By supporting the aims of national educational strategies, whilst remaining flexible within a fluid system, such learning resources encourage children to learn about their nation's history, whilst also contributing to towards their development as individuals. The Prestonpans Tapestry offers learning opportunities which are both informal and formal, for schools and parents alike, cross-curricular and cross-generational. The Prestonpans Tapestry will surely prove itself to be an integral asset for the preservation and promotion of Scotland's national heritage, and the smaller details of which it is composed.

It's all in the detail . . .

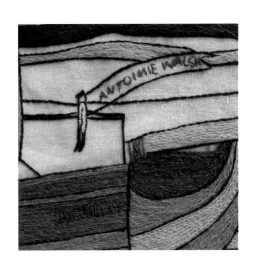

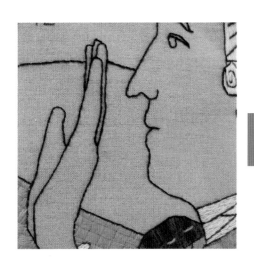

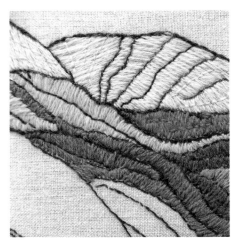

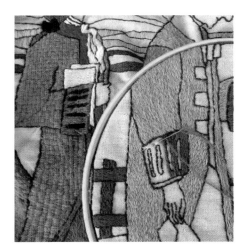

The Prestonpans Tapestry – Hope Ambition and Victory!

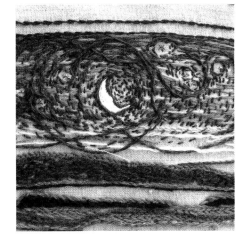

The Prestonpans Tapestry – Hope Ambition and Victory!

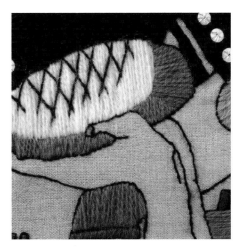

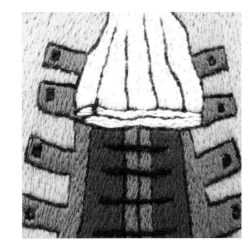

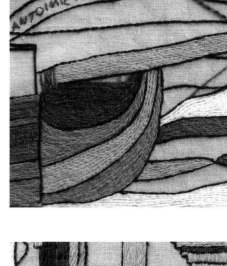

The Stitchers Roll

"Working together has its own creative magic – and it's fun!"

by Gordon Prestoungrange

There are already at least three story lines in circulation about The Prestonpans Tapestry. The first is that it tells of the young Prince's determination to regain his father's kingdom, which of course it does. Less obviously, it evidences the determination of the post-industrial community in Prestonpans since 1997 to recover its sense of place *through the arts* after the collapse of its socioeconomic fabric in the 1960s and the Battle in September 1745 is a significant element of that sense of place. The third story line tells of the Herculean volunteer 'stitchers' who created a tapestry's 104 one metre panels, the longest in the world, in the space of nine months – that third story is now beginning to emerge – and here's a first summary.

Best estimates, since not even our self-confessed 'diarist' stitcher in Eskbank was actually counting, suggest more than 10 million stitches were made over 25,000 hours. There was no apparent organisation structure for what has been accomplished, just an invitation to volunteer, a drop-in-centre, a website and a midway share-and-compare workshop. Certainly the 1745 cartoon of Cope confirming his own defeat at Prestonpans to Lord Ker in Berwick had been taken as the 'design' concept

by artist Andrew Crummy, the initial 79 panels had been identified from the many written accounts of the Prince's campaign, and suitable wools and linen had been found. But virtually everything else has been heuristic. It just simply emerged as volunteers arrived, offering ideas and skill and time and support and encouragement. The leadership that arose was situational. There were no elections to roles as they became necessary, they were just assumed and welcomed whether that role was doing further research on the content of panels or the architecture of the mid 18th century, in helping finish panels where an original volunteer was unable, in blocking, photographing and stitching the panels together as fives. The project's excitement and dynamic simply created volunteers, all sorts and conditions of people literally across the world wanted to be part of it. To be of it and in it became and remained an exhilarating experience – despite some natural angst and the looming deadlines.

"... skills learned from grandmother and mother ...."

The majority of the talented embroiderers who stitched The Prestonpans Tapestry gained their interest and their skills in sewing from grandmother

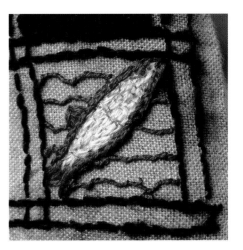

or mother, although in two moving instances the skill was acquired whilst convalescing from TB as a child, one taught by nuns. For a minority there was almost a complete lack of experience at sewing much more than buttons on school uniforms but there was amongst them all a cadre with a very great deal of experience, often with hard won City & Guilds or Art College qualifications in embroidery and textile design, several of whom were teachers in these fields. Many too were members of arts and crafts groups such as the Halflinbarns Schoolhouse Weavers, the Embroiders Guild, the Scottish Costume Society, the Craft Clinic in Fisherrow, the Inveresk Sewers, the Culrose Needlwork Group and the Stathendrick Stitchers. Other groups were non-specific but resolved to tackle panels such as Ageing Well Edinburgh and the Scottish Rurals WI.

One of the most fascinating aspects of those who volunteered however was not the variety of their competence or skills but their declared motivations for wanting to take part. High amongst them was a love of Scotland, 'doing something for Scotland' one declared. Equally there were deep Jacobite emotions usually with strong ancestral connections. The Prince had lodged in 1745 in more than one of the stitchers' ancestral family homes such as Gray's Mill and Sunlaws close by Kelso. And where there might be no direct link there were myriad instances of nostalgic or highly localised associations. Dunblane's stitchers took the greatest interest in Balhaldie House and those on Eriskay and living in and close by Kinlochmoidart House were determined to sew 'their' panels. The parents of the stitcher of the Salutation Inn in Perth had met, held their wedding reception and ruby wedding celebrations in that very hotel. Another's ancestors had tended the Light at Ardnamurchan not long after the Prince had sailed in its surrounding waters. Robertsons were determined to stitch the panel for Blair Castle and the capture of Cope's coach at Cockenzie. Eponymous Andersons wished to stitch the Riggonhead Defile and those whose homes today are depicted in the Inveresk panel wished to stitch them. The Craft Clinic at Fisherrow, having resolved to tackle the two Musselburgh panels including Pinkie House, found their neighbour at the Craft Clinic actually stayed in Pinkie House today and recruited her to stitch her own bedroom window.

Yet how did all these stitchers hear about, learn about the tapestry project in the first place? The first occasion the Trust 'asked' for volunteers was on the rear cover of the 2009 3Harbours Festival programme – in May/ June. That proved decisive, not only bringing forward the first dozen or more volunteers but those early volunteers were very frequently members of the arts and crafts groups already mentioned. There was immediate clamour for the panels to stitch which couldn't be met that swiftly, but workshops were held at the Prestoungrange Gothenburg for the ever increasing number of volunteers to share Andrew Crummy's earliest drawings and to ask for their critique. Many stitchers began to reserve particular panels for the manner of reasons already described. But the Trustees definitely wanted to encourage stitchers right across the Highlands not just close by in the Lowlands. A grand expedition was planned to Eriskay plus a week's residence at Borrodale. The Trust's BattleBus took to the road and with the help of press coverage in *Am Paipear* and *Westword* stitchers were found at presentations in Eriskay & Astley Halls, by door stepping at Kinlochmoidart and in car park chatter at Glenfinnan. Local Highland weekly newspapers also carried the call for

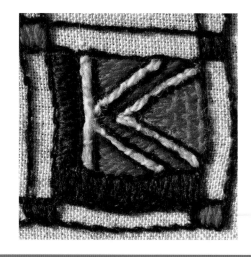

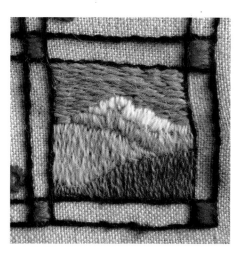

"Working together has its own creative magic – and it's fun!"

volunteers as did *The Scotsman*, the *East Lothian Courier, Life* and *News*. And of course there were exceptional word-of-mouth recruits. A volunteer from the USA was a longstanding family friend of a Port Seton stitcher who'd gone to Florida as a Rotary Ambassador, from Australia a migrant mother was alerted by her Musselburgh daughter, in Dublin the artist's father-in-law and at Feuillade in France this book's graphic designer's family and expat circle signed on. To our absolute delight by Christmas 2009 we knew we had more than enough stitchers to accomplish the challenge – indeed there were reserves to spare.

"Panel Beaters, stitch addicts watched over by husbands and cats ..."

Several were alpha women, but they did not dominate and with only the rarest exception did they remonstrate. Their contributions were deployed quietly and effectively co-ordinating dispersed sub-sets of stitchers and helping show 'how' at the drop-in sessions. They were indispensable. But so were the contributions of the angels who were always there quietly helping and when needed stepping up to the breach or stitching the way out of a tight corner. More than one volunteer had to admit they could not finish on time or as well as they felt they should, and the quiet ones quietly did what was needed.

As the project progressed nick names emerged and were adopted. The core team proclaimed they were 'panel beaters' whilst individual stitchers admitted to becoming stitch addicts or junkies with earnest discussion of detox routines. 'Some weeks I couldn't put it down, other weeks I couldn't pick it up'. 'Lemsip Linda' had to start her tapestry panel all over when she spilt the medicine on her linen! Others more prosaically talked of 'stitching during the long winter months' – and it was a tough winter, whilst a poet amongst them mused: 'stitching frees yet challenges the mind'. Habitual behaviours developed – one group that could have imbibed whisky galore opted to take Earl Grey tea; another ate McGhee's cakes when they met every Tuesday. Others reported just how far their panels had travelled, not only on holidays to France or Norfolk but to Glen Nevis and Portsoy – the latter when a coterie of Port Seton & Cockenzie stitchers became obsessed with rowing their *Boatie Blest*, their crews becoming 2010 World Champions in their class!

Husbands [all but one stitcher were female] came in for many a compliment, and sympathy, as did the occasional cat and dog. All watched patiently and husbands attended to domestic duties many stitchers would normally have done. Fellow embroiderers were greatly valued for their mutual contributions, suggesting stitching ideas, showing what they'd achieved as exemplars at the Thursday drop-in and Midway workshops. The website also played a significant role here even though only two thirds of stitchers were au fait with the technology.

"But where were the moon and the stars?"

All stitchers were determined to get 'their panel' as right as may be and from the outset were very much encouraged to do so.. Andrew Crummy and his history counsellors had done their best but ....? Perhaps the most spectacular instance of correctly second guessing was at Blair Castle where the Roberstons had the panel in hand. The Prince stayed several days watching bowls and evidently eating his first pineapple. There are several stories of his sojourn but few gave proper precedence to the exiled Jacobite William, Duke of Atholl and his cousin Lady Lude – who organised a Ball. Another stitcher was greatly taxed as to the position in the sky of the moon and the stars on September 20th/ 21st. No less an authority than the French Astronomical Society was successfully consulted. At Glenfinnan debate raged, and remains unresolved, as to where precisely the Prince's Standard was raised. The present Cameron of Lochiel [a Founding Patron of the Battle Trust] was consulted and added a stitch or two to the panel himself. At Dunbar the stitcher's husband was despatched to the harbour to locate 'Cope's Steps' which he successfully did; at Fassfern the bedroom where the Prince slept was explored to see just how easily he could have plucked the iconic white rose outside the window. Others, as on Eriskay,

questioned and corrected the disposition of the islands offshore, and yet more adjusted the architecture of the buildings.

Alas it's finished!

This community 'arts' project, creating the world's longest tapestry, occasioned virtually all the benefits one could have anticipated. For some it provided an absorbing opportunity to sideline just a little a current sadness or to distract a tad from a debilitating illness. Its momentum and the sheer beauty of what was emerging raised the spirits and the souls of all concerned. Elderly mothers and daughters worked together on panels, in one case mother was losing her sight but she certainly made her contribution. Grandchildren watched, often puzzled but receiving unthought of lessons in Scottish history, and many added a stitch or two. Everyone said they couldn't wait to see it finished and that they desperately wanted to see the entire tapestry once it was stitched together. They'd fly in from America, or Australia, Ireland or France, or descend from the Highlands to the Lowlands, for that sight. A 'private viewing' all together, for everyone who stitched, was a must. So was this book of the Tapestry as a keepsake and souvenir – not incidentally that the photographic images on these pages so carefully prepared by Gillian Hart can ever match the depth and texture of the embroidered linen. Embroidery is a unique medium, but this book tries to offer what the panels alone cannot, the rounded story.

Because we all recognise the uniqueness of embroidery as a medium the Trust further resolved that the real McCoy must be toured, paraded across

the nation and in due course the Diaspora. It was resolved to carry it across the Highlands in triumph to the very places the Prince visited in 1745 on the very dates he was there. It had to travel to Eriskay and Arisaig and Glenfinnan and Fort William [true the Prince never took that Fort!], to Blair Castle, Perth, Dunblane and Sterling. And in each of these locations the stitchers' friends and family and their local communities will be able to see what together 'they' have accomplished, and perhaps learn a little more of their history. And the simple message is that so very much can be achieved by 'voluntarism'. What we behold is quite simply astonishing, amazing, incredible.

Legacies from the Legacy

At the Battle Trust we anticipate six major outcomes, legacies of our legacy from the Prince. First and foremost we expect to heighten national awareness of, and thereby advance, our campaign to create a vibrant Living History Centre in Prestonpans with the Tapestry as a prime exhibit. Secondly, we expect to see a surge of interest in and involvement with sewing/ stitching/ embroidery. Seeing what has been achieved will certainly trigger ideas and aspirations amongst others to create a similarly beautiful artwork. Thirdly we expect to see the Tapestry visited by a host of young students as they study the Scottish History curriculum with it becoming a powerful new medium that supplements the Trust's existing programme of re-enactments and BattleGaming. Fourthly, we expect debate and disagreement and learning all around from the details we have placed in the Tapestry's panels and our history notes – the story of the '45 is so replete with romanticised myth that we have no illusions we have it all right – only Allah is Perfect! Fifthly, we shall trumpet the triumph of 'voluntarism'. It can move mountains – of linen and wool – and it can move hearts and minds. And sixthly, we expect to see a greater surge in the continuing re-assertion of our community self-esteem in Prestonpans and our neighbours in Port Seton and Cockenzie, through the arts, as we all make our way in the 21st century. There is every right to be immensely proud of the sense of place our heritage has afforded our community – not only arising from this iconic battle in 1745 but from The Pans' industrial contribution to the Scottish nation across a thousand years.

10 million thanks to everyone who stitched a stitch and to everyone who made their stitching possible.

Panel Index to Events Described & Principal Actors